FRACTAL ARCHITECTURE:
DESIGN FOR SUSTAINABILITY

the collaboration on saving the planet

Kenneth Haggard
&
Polly Cooper

with assistance from Christine Gyovai

First published in the United States of America in 2006 by
BookSurge Publishing, 7290 B Investment Drive
North Charleston, SC 29418

Library of Congress Cataloging-in-Publication Data
Haggard, Kenneth L., M. Polly Cooper and Christine Gyovai
Fractal Architecture: Design for Sustainability
p.cm
Includes bibliographical references and index.
ISBN: 1-4196-2469-5 (softcover)

1. Environmental Design. 2. Architectural design.
3. Sustainability. 4. Aesthetics
2006908486

A portion of the proceeds from the sale of this book will be donated to
the nonprofit organization California ReLeaf to support the planting of
trees to help offset the trees that were used in the creation of this book.
For more information, go to the website: www.californiareleaf.org

This book is dedicated to:

Antonio Gaudi	Spain
Hector Guimard	France
Rene McIntosh and Mary McDonald	UK
Frank Lloyd Wright	USA

Five giants of the formative phase of Industrial Era design 100 years ago whose great examples of integration pointed the way.

FOREWORD

This foreword is being written in Canopy Tower at the edge of the Soberania National Park rainforest preserve in Panama. Canopy Tower was built as a radar platform in 1964 by the United States as part of the air defense system of the Panama Canal, and was refurbished in 1988 to help intercept airborne cocaine smugglers from Columbia. It was included in the facilities handed over to the Republic of Panama in 1995 as part of the Carter-Torrijos Treaties that returned the Canal to Panama after eighty years of United States control. In 1998 it was leased by Raul Arias de Para to be remodeled into a lodge. In 1999, Canopy Tower was opened as an eco-tourist facility. When standing on the upper level of this five-story tower an observer is at the same level as the canopy of the rainforest. The moving monoliths of container ships plying the Canal are visible to the southwest, as well as the skyline of modern Panama City to the southeast. From this view, in one spectacular panorama, striking examples of the three main subjects of this book are visible.

First is the environment of the surrounding forest. Here we can interact with brightly colored birds, six-inch iridescent blue moths that strobe their way through the trees, and see occasional rainforest mammals such as sloths and coatis. We can hear the distant roar of howler monkeys and choruses of birds, frogs and insects. These rainforests are among the world's richest, most diverse ecosystems, and are among the most threatened. Being here is a vivid reminder of why sustainability is so crucial to our time.

Second, there is the Canal—one of the greatest examples of engineering and construction of the early industrial era. Prior to building, a large pubic health effort was undertaken to eradicate the scourge of yellow fever, which had stopped an earlier effort by the French to build the Canal. Mountains were leveled and vast lakes created to provide water to serve its great locks. The Canal also required the construction of elaborate defenses, of which the Tower is a small part. This vast intrusion of human works into the landscape continues to expand today as the Canal is widened.

Third, there is the modern city seen from its most romantic viewpoint, a tight packet of towers on the horizon behind layers of forested mountains. From this view it appears as any modern industrial city, sitting in splendid isolation from its surroundings. It is the industrial city emerging from the older, agriculturally based colonial city that cannot be seen from this distance. As with all cities, it must become an emerging sustainable city where the surrounding environment, our elaborate technology, and the built environment are reconciled.

On a smaller scale, the architecture of this former radar tower vividly expresses this emergence. In spite of (or perhaps because of) its history, the observation tower seems to serve its present function better than if it had originally been designed for this purpose. It sits high on a hilltop providing the canopy view and access to breezes so critical for human comfort in a successful passively cooled building in this tropical climate. The dome gives shade from the intense sun on some part of the observation deck at any time of the day. The night lighting is all yellow light (except in the bathrooms) so as not to overly disrupt the unimaginably intricate insect life that is such an important part of the rainforest. The Tower recycles water from the bathrooms for gardens at the base, and to flush toilets when well water is scarce during the dry season.

In addition to all this, the Tower's architecture is symbolic—symbolic in that it is an instrument of war recycled into an instrument of peace. Peace, not just between potentially warring nations, but peace between nature and humankind. In the long run, this is a far more important peace—one that is necessary for our survival and one that can only be achieved by a practical working reconciliation of our threatened environments, our massive technical abilities and our ubiquitous architecture, via sustainable design.

before renovation

after renovation

sitting, dining and library

observation

bedrooms

bedrooms

entry and forest exhibit

Illustration A-1 -- Canopy Tower Lodge in Panama

2 *(photos by Raul Arias de Para - owner of the Canopy Lodge)*

STRUCTURE OF THIS BOOK

Words, words, words. We inhabit a culture that is dominated by the abstraction of the written word. Words make sentences, which in turn make paragraphs, chapters, and finally, books. The underlying structure and use of written language is linear, with the mind and memory of the reader acting as integrator. This structure served us well in the development of science and industry with their emphasis on reductionism and linear thinking. However, with the need for holistic and integrated thinking, we have progressively given more prominence to other forms of graphic communication, including the chemically/mechanically aided graphic imagery of photographs and movies and the more recent development of electronically aided imagery using icons to facilitate human interface with computer programs.

This book uses some of these different approaches to expedite communication and make integrated relationships more explicit. Thus, a great deal of emphasis will be given to pictures, diagrams, icons and symbols as defined in the diagram below. This diagram compares these different types of graphic communication arranged in a spectrum from less abstract to more abstract.

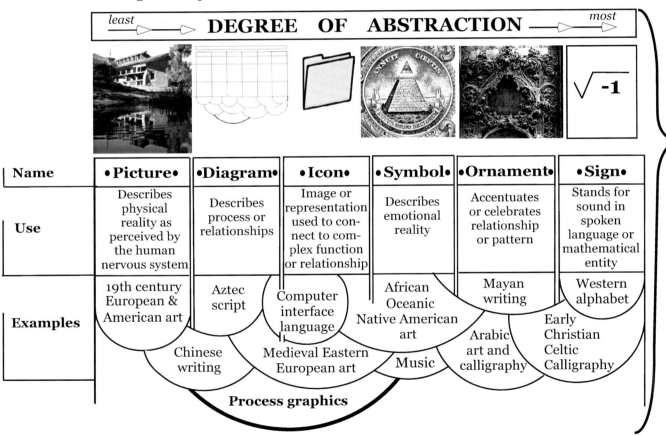

Illustration A-2 -- Spectrum of graphic types

Because sustainability and fractal geometry involve process and relationship, this book will rely on diagrams overlapping into pictures and symbols as indicated on the part of this illustration titled **process graphics**.

The index on pages 5 and 6 is an example. It attempts, by taking a diagrammatic form, to do more than just show the parts of this book and on what page each part can be found. It is also meant to show some of the iterative structural patterns of the whole and the relationships between parts.

The advantages of using this approach may be seen by comparing Illustration A-2 to a written version of the same information shown below. The point is that writing is generally better for depth but slower for structural relationships because integration—a view of the whole picture—is implicit. In process graphics, structural ideas are perceived faster because integration is explicit. Detail is harder to develop than with alphabetic writing, although relationships and patterns are more obvious.[1]

There are six types of graphic communication which are differentiated by their degree of abstraction. The first is the **picture**, the second is the **diagram**, the third is the **icon**, the forth is the **symbol**, the fifth is **ornament**, and the sixth is **letters** and **signs**. *Pictures* are graphics that illustrate reality as perceived by the human nervous system and usually involve techniques that enhance visual realism such as rules of perspective and proportion. *Diagrams* describe process or relationships between parts of a larger whole and are concerned with describing systems or flows of materials or energy. *Icons* are an image or symbolic representation of complex relationships and are used to interface the user to a larger reality. *Symbols* describe emotional reality and can be powerful at the subconscious level. A picture can be used metaphorically so that it becomes a symbol. A diagram further abstracted can also become a symbol—religious symbols are some of the most common. *Ornament* accentuates or celebrates relationship or pattern. Ornaments can be abstracted to the point where meaning is subordinated to decorative use. *Letters and signs* stand for spoken sound (in the Western alphabet) or for mathematical entities and relationships.

To help clarify these types we can look at some historical examples. Traditional Western art, with few exceptions, tends to emphasize the picture. This reached its height in the 19th century when much accepted art, including ornament, was pictorial. This was practiced to such an extreme that the rich diagrammatic and symbolic art of Africa, Oceania and Native America was relegated to the category of "primitive art." In the late 19th century, Western art started expanding beyond the pictorial into diagrammatic and symbolic art inspired by nature. This was a precursor to the temporary overthrow of realism in the early 20th century by "modern art"—art that defiantly sought a greater degree of abstraction, which in some circles was called "abstract art." Suddenly, the so-called "primitive art" of previous cultures became valued as inspiration for modern artists.

Islamic art took a totally different approach. Because of the religious proscription against graven images, Islamic artists developed a rich and sophisticated art form based on abstract ornament. Much of this ornament used the Arabic alphabet and literal quotes from the Koran. It also employed abstract geometrical forms in repetitive ornamental ways, at times approaching the level of complexity found in fractal geometry. Early Christian Celtic calligraphy, though more pictorially based, was similar in its rich ornamental basis.

Icons, such as images of saints or other religious figures, were the foundation of much medieval art in Eastern Europe. The importance of icons became so profound that fiercely fought conflicts occurred between the devotees of icons and those who felt that the use of icons was too image-oriented and thus idolatrous (the iconoclasts). We use icons today to represent complex relationships such as the interface between users and computer software. As a result, icons have again become common.

Chinese characters used for writing are another interesting historical example. They evolved from combining pictograms, a form of picture writing, with ideograms, the use of diagrams. There are other interesting examples that show other degrees of emphasis. Aztec script, like Chinese, was a combination of pictures as ideograms but used in completely different ways.

For these reasons, this book puts as much emphasis on process graphics and page composition as writing in an effort to benefit from the speed of sight as well as the slower speed of reading. Faster communication of integral relationships is one aspect of "miniaturization"—a recurring theme in this book (see page 21)—and an important aspect of sustainability.

---

[1] A highly provocative history of the cultural effects of writing and literacy, both negative and positive, are developed in Leonard Shlain's *The Alphabet Versus the Goddess: The Conflict Between Word and Image*, Penguin Compass, 1998.

This book consists of Section I. OVERVIEW, but implies the structure shown in Section II. ENVIRONMENTAL DESIGN. Section II. can be thought of as a sequel or a suggestion for the reader to build upon.

II. ENVIRONMENTAL DESIGN

C. FRACTAL SCALES OF DESIGN

	1. Bioclimatic Scales	2. Settlement Pattern Scales	3. Architectural Scales	4. Artifact Scales
a. Introduction	biome bioregion watershed communities	vernacular classical industrial sustainable	metabolism & form function, flow and complexity location & materials aesthetics & expression	need and product product infrastructure symbolism and scale cultural effects
b. tools	Natural History- processes & forms	Cultural History- processes & forms	Fractal enfoldment as a design process	Fractal functionalism as a design process
c. approaches	bioclimatic design permaculture regenerative design	new urbanism cohousing advocacy and green planning	solar architecture fractal architecture green architecture	ecological design appropriate technology green products
d. processes			Each scale of concern is enfolded with all the others, regardless of the actual size of the project.	
e. examples				

D. FRACTAL DESIGN

INTRODUCTION TO CONCEPTS SECTION

A conceptual image of the world, sophisticated or crude, explicit or implied, is the glue that holds a society together and provides the intellectual energy that drives it. Even the briefest look at history will reveal how diverse human constructions of a worldview can be. The old adage, "the universe is infinitely capable of adapting itself to your version of reality," seems to hold true. Anthropology reveals an amazing variety of worldview concepts that have been developed within the universality of being human. We have a rich heritage of incredible sophistication of language, literature, ritual, technology, art and architecture that have been used to express and maintain these conceptual models.

Imagine trying to compare the conceptual worldview of a minor priest in Tenochtitlan (now Mexico City) in 1500 with that of a minor executive today. Tenochtitlan was the capital of a far-flung empire about the size of France. The priest lived in what appeared to be a floating city, but was actually a tight pattern of agricultural *chinampas*.[2] This city of 150,000 - 250,000 people was the largest city in the Americas, larger than any European city at that time. Much of the economy was based on tribute and protected trade, resulting in a level of prosperity previously unknown in this region. Almost daily this priest participated in human sacrifice to the dual gods of Uitzilopochtli and Tlaloc. This man probably had as elaborate a worldview as the mid-level executive of today who works, isolated from nature, in an air-conditioned high rise building, planning the sacrifice of some ecosystem to the dual gods of Growth and Gain.

To make things even more complex, these conceptual views play out in a chaotically patterned environment of evolution and change. Sometimes this change is catastrophic, as it was in the brittle state of Tenochtitlan in 1521 when it was destroyed by Cortez's army of Spaniards, Indians and the smallpox virus they introduced.

Artist: Thomas Buchanan
<u>Illustration A-3 -- Tenochtitlan from surrounding hills around 1500 A.D.</u>

[2] A highly productive system of marshland agriculture developed in the lake where the Aztecs were forced to live when they first entered the valley, thus turning adversity to their advantage.

An argument can be made that all the past conceptual modes are still with us. In this view, society is like a pond where on the calm surface we find the predominating, generally accepted social mores and beliefs. Below the surface, at different levels, is all the diversity of which humans have been capable. In the muck at the bottom one can find the most conflicting (and often destructive) beliefs that have been normative at other periods of history. This includes beliefs dominated by violence, murder and torture-- essentially all that the term 'evil' describes and of which we are all capable. Evolution and change is inherent in our environment. However, if change is catastrophic, the murky depths can be stirred and these destructive forces come to the surface as they did in the 1930s in Central Europe, the 1970s in Cambodia, the 1980s in Argentina, and at the beginning of our new century in Oklahoma City, New York and Baghdad.

Sustainability, besides producing healthier, richer, and more truly productive physical and cultural environments, reduces the chance of such destructive catastrophic change.

Society is a living organism constructed of concepts. Whether concepts become food, medicine, disease, drugs, madness or cure depends upon a very complex interplay in the culture. Therefore, it is important to participate in the evolution of conceptual frameworks. **For our time and place, developing the concepts of sustainability and the geometry of sustainable design is vital.** These are the two subjects of this section.

**Illustration A-4 -- Tenochtitan 1500 A.D.
Los Angeles 2006 A.D.**

8

SUSTAINABILITY OFFERS GREATER, NOT LESSER, WEALTH.
SUSTAINABLE DESIGN CAN HELP OPTIMIZE DIVERSE
GOALS LIKE HEALTH, WEALTH AND EQUITY.

A.1 SUSTAINABILITY
a. definitions

Sustainability was defined at the United Nations Conference on the Environment in 1994 as "the ability to meet the needs of the present without compromising the needs of future generations." In *The Ecology of Commerce,* author Paul Hawken states that sustainability will be "the next phase of the Industrial Revolution." Definitions are important, but we need to recognize their elusiveness in such large-scale concerns. Using one word as a symbol to address multiple values and modes of change creates as much ambiguity as other word-symbols such as God, Patriotism, Beauty, Freedom, Progress and Love that are also difficult to define and yet have become the basis of great human endeavor.

While the United Nations definition is the most generally accepted, it isn't specific enough to act as a good working definition. To be more precise, an adequate definition of sustainability must recognize that the environment and human activity are an interconnected, co-evolutionary whole. It is not just the protection of the environment that defines sustainability. It is also a new level of perception, design and enterprise based on the perception of humans as an important part of our planet's processes. Our part in these processes must become more optimal in order to sustain ourselves, other species, and the planet.

It is helpful to develop a working definition around which multidisciplinary design teams can communicate. A single definition won't do because sustainability is both simple and complex. We found it helpful as designers to define sustainability with a spectrum of definitions from simplest to most complex as shown below.

SUSTAINABILITY

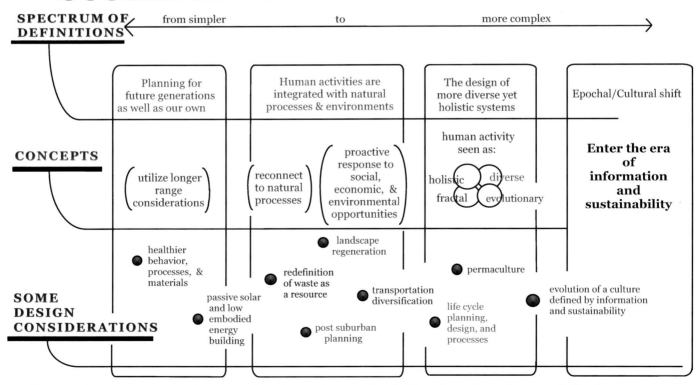

**Illustration A-5 -- Working definition of sustainability for planning and design purposes
San Luis Sustainability Group Architects**

A.1 SUSTAINABILITY
b. Conceptual implications and problems

If sustainability is part of an epochal/cultural shift as shown on the right side of Illustration A-5, the greatest barrier to understanding sustainability is residual biases from the preceding era. It is just as difficult for us to imagine what a sustainable culture might be as it was for our ancestors to try to envision a scientific and industrial culture when their known cultural concepts were those of agriculture and husbandry. These difficulties often lead to philosophical traps that need to be carefully examined. Some of the most common traps are related to the following questions: our place in nature, human population growth, achieving environmental balance and modifying our use of resources.

The question of our place in nature. Many people share a hopeless feeling that we as a species are bad for the environment. It is as if we are cursed with an ecological version of original sin. Humans are detrimental to nature—a species out of control—guilty just by being. This view asserts that we must sacrifice to atone for being. We must use less of everything, and we should be righteous enough to do with less and be happy. There is enough truth in this approach to make it insidious. In reality, we *are* out of control—at least our industrial society is. We are wasting our resources and our future. Things need to change, but are guilt and righteousness the best mechanisms? Before we examine the fallacies of this approach, it is important to recognize where these concepts come from. This lonely separation of our species into reflexive guilt, sacrifice and righteous atonement is a reappearance of the Puritanism that was an integral part of the beginning of the Industrial Revolution.

There has been much discussion regarding the social circumstances that set the stage for the Industrial Revolution. These circumstances involved three seemingly unrelated social movements. First, Western Monasticism rationalized time by inventing clocks, imposing strict schedules, and promulgating a particular version of time separate from the time of natural processes like diurnal cycles and seasons. Then Puritanism convinced many people to give up the pleasures of the present for expectations in the future to atone for original sin. This lead to the idea of saving and investment that was critical in the creation of a job-based economy. Third was the development of an intellectual culture during the Renaissance and later the Enlightenment that emphasized the material, secular and worldly, and encouraged exploration, invention and scientific inquiry. This strange and often contradictory brew of religious, cultural, and social ideas created conceptual conditions in Europe that allowed for the birth of the Industrial Revolution.[3] But now we are at the beginning of the next stage of cultural evolution. Many of the attitudes that were an integral part of the previous evolution are no longer helpful.

The fallacy of perceiving humans as separate from nature is that it confuses humankind with a particular cultural era. Humankind is an evolving species; the industrial culture is only one phase in this evolution. Commonly, we fail to differentiate between ourselves as a species and our particular cultural phase and we *overdifferentiate* between the natural world and ourselves. The idea that we are inherently separate from nature is an industrial-era mind-set and is an assumption we must grow out of. It is true that humankind has been incredibly destructive, but wallowing in guilt takes valuable energy that is needed to create a new cultural era that is more constructive and less destructive to us and our planet.

---

[3] Many scientific discoveries and industrial processes were achieved in China, the world's most technologically advanced county in the 15th century. However, a strict policy of isolation beginning in 1433 along with other factors, allowed Europe to bypass China on the way to the Industrial Revolution. This is further discussed by John Merson in *The Genius That Was China: East and West in the Making of the Modern World,* Overlook Press, 1998.

The question of population growth. Of the four questions we are concerned with here--our place in nature, human population growth, achieving environmental balance, and our use of resources--population growth seems to be the most enervating. As with the previous question, at first glance a sense of hopelessness is the common response. Plotting human population growth on a graph shows an exponential growth rate where, for example, from 1950 - 2000, China's population grew by more people than existed in the entire world at the start of the Industrial Revolution. As the preeminent biologist Edward O. Wilson put it, "The pattern of human population growth in the 20th century was more bacterial than primate." Again, as in the previous question, many people stop here and give up the question in despair. Many environmentally concerned people believe there should be zero population growth, but also feel it is impossible to achieve.

Like the problem of our place in nature, it is necessary to look deeper into this question. Are there patterns within population growth that we are not seeing? There are if we look at the situation in a different way. In dealing with non-linear conditions like pH in chemistry, earthquake magnitudes in geology or population dynamics, a linear graph as in Illustration A-6 is not very informative beyond a very gross level. However, if we plot human population growth logarithmically (in other words, nonlinearly), we get a different product. The result shown in Illustration A-7.

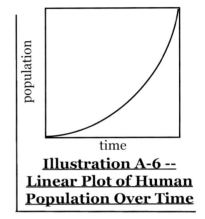

Illustration A-6 -- Linear Plot of Human Population Over Time

This chart[4] shows growth rate, but also illustrates nuances about relative growth rates at various times. Each "bump" shown is a cultural era.

1. the era of hunting and gathering (era 1)
2. the era of agriculture and husbandry (era 2)
3. the era of science and industry (era 3)

This chart will be referenced throughout this book because of what it reveals about where we've been and where we are headed (see pages 89 - 94 and 122). For now, it is enough to introduce the chart in the discussion of the question of population growth.

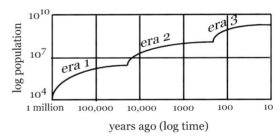

Illustration A-7 -- Log Scale Plot of Human Population Over Time

It can be seen that each era consists of relatively steep and relatively flat areas of growth. In the flat areas, growth still occurs, but at a significantly slower rate. What does this chart and other, more in-depth information tell us? The stages of population growth level off appreciably at the end of each era. In this regard, we find that zero population growth has already occurred in many industrialized countries (era 3 shown at the right end of the curve). In his latest book, *The Future of Life*, Edward O. Wilson states that by the year 2000 the replacement rate in all the countries of western Europe had dropped below 2.1, with the lead taken by Italy at 1.2 children per woman.[5]

[4] Robert R. Cates, "Sustaining Life on Earth," *Scientific American* (October 1994): 114-122.
[5] Edward O. Wilson, *The Future of Life*. New York: Alfred Knopf, 2003.

Both Thailand and the non-immigrant population of the United States have achieved this magic number, and in fact some countries, like Italy and Germany, have entered a period of negative population growth.

If this is the case, why is there still such anxiety about population pressure? The answer lies in the pre- and semi-industrial world, which contains the majority of the world's population, and is not at the same phase of development as the industrialized countries. There is a lag between the transition from Era 2 to Era 3, and the steep part of the curve in Era 3. In Era 2 cultures, large families are desirable and generally necessary due to high infant mortality rates, the need for many hands to help farm and for assurance of care in old age. In industrialized countries, Edward O. Wilson argues,

> "The freeing of women socially and economically results in fewer children. Reduced reproduction by female choice can be thought a fortunate, indeed almost miraculous, gift of human nature to future generations. It could have gone the other way: women, more prosperous and less shackled, could have chosen the satisfaction of a larger brood. They did the opposite. They opted for a smaller number of quality children, who can be raised with better health and education, over a larger family. They simultaneously chose better, more secure lives for themselves. The tendency appears to be very widespread, if not universal. Its importance cannot be overstated. Social commentators often remark that humanity is endangered by its own instincts, such as tribalism, aggression, and personal greed. Demographers of the future will, I believe, point out that on the other hand humanity was saved by this one quirk in the maternal instinct."[6]

Other factors affecting population growth in industrial countries, aside from the positive one mentioned above, include the more frantic pace of life, less cohesive family units and endocrine-effecting pollutants that make reproduction and child-rearing a more complex situation. Yet population in the U.S., especially in California, is increasing rapidly. This is due to migration from largely Era 2 transition cultures in Latin America and elsewhere. A similar increase in western Europe is the result of people migrating from North African countries, while in eastern Europe immigrants from the Middle East contribute to population growth. Besides direct migration, these new arrivals have traditionally produced larger families until they become assimilated into the industrialized culture. These migrations are largely the result of inequalities between Era 2 and Era 3 cultures caused by the exploitation policies of the industrial countries in the 19th and 20th centuries. One could mention Karmic justice or Jesus' admonishment, "The meek shall inherit the Earth." An interesting illustration of this situation in California can be found in an increase in the percentage of Native Americans. This is not the same group of Native Americans that were so oppressed in the 19th century. Much of the increase is Native Americans from Mexico, which in the historical context, was the center of population concentrations in pre-Columbian America.

Population growth is a serious problem, but conditions are not totally hopeless. Solutions are complex and involve achieving more equity worldwide. Thus social justice and equity must by necessity be integral components of sustainability.

---

[6] Edward O. Wilson, *The Future of Life.* New York: Alfred Knopf, 2003.

The question of environmental balance. Another basic question that is seemingly simple but is fraught with conceptual problems is that of balance. Our first impulse may be to believe that balance must be achieved between humans and nature, our appetites and impact, and our economy and ecology. Again there is enough truth in this position to give this notion a lot of power. Certainly much of the industrial era has progressed with very little thought for consequences. This has resulted in an out-of-control juggernaut of unhealthy and destructive imbalances and unsustainable practices. The effects of these practices are now well documented. One effort to understand these effects is the concept of the "ecological footprint" developed by Mathis Wackernagel and William Rees.[7] Wackernagel and Rees determine the impact of our way of living through the amount of land it takes to maintain present industrial lifestyles. This accounting system vividly illustrates the unsustainable character of so much of the way we live in industrial societies that it is easy to be swept into the crusade for balance. But we must be careful about how we define balance to avoid being caught again in outdated definitions and attitudes. Balance is often defined by a rigorous accounting of inputs and outputs across the boundaries of a closed system that can be quantified. A system can be called balanced when these inputs and outputs are equal. Elaborate accounting of this type is being refined by Mathis Wackernagel, Greg Norris, Pliny Fisk and others into useful tools for developing measuring systems for sustainable economics.

As useful as these conceptual devices are, we must watch out for several theoretical problems. One is the idea of homeostasis, or static balance. This type of balance is at the heart of industrial concepts. If a system can be set up so that it can be maintained without variation, where all change can be eliminated, then a highly efficient industrial process is possible. This is, in a way, the Holy Grail of the passing industrial culture, and is the foundation of the monocultures that it produces so readily. Outcomes such as the horrors of factory farming, the banality of suburban housing and the monotony of assembly lines can all be attributed to this agenda. The problem is that reality, especially the reality of living organisms, is never truly static. Really important things, whether ecological systems, landscapes or heartbeats, all dance to a complex, collective and chaotic rhythm—"chaotic" in the modern scientific sense of unpredictable variations within prescribed limits, not in the literary sense of fearful disorder.

An everyday example can illustrate this notion. The question of human comfort demonstrates how important the distinction is between balance that is static and balance that is chaotically rhythmic. Humans evolved in environments that varied in temperature, humidity, wind conditions, etc. This is made more complex by taking into account activity level, particular clothing, state of mind, mood, etc. With the development of heating and cooling of buildings by mechanical systems (completed after 1950 with the mass application of air conditioning), ideal standards were determined to balance thermal extremes to achieve comfort. This approach to thermal control occurred during the Classical period of the industrial era (for a definition, see page 92) in North America—therefore the industrial bias of homeostasis was applied. The ideal temperature was considered to be 72°F and mechanical systems were designed with the idea of making the balance between cold and hot as constant as possible. This led to the ideal shown in Illustration A-8, with "design temperature" being tightly defined. In the 1960s, this resulted in the extreme of building elementary schools that were windowless boxes to maximize the efficiencies of air conditioning systems, while completely ignoring the organic complexities of the children and teachers by eliminating any outside views of daylight, seasons, nature or site. This was quite unfortunate because in these schools, people were treated as mechanisms rather than organisms, in the name of human comfort.

---

[7] Mathis Wackernagel and William Rees, *Our Ecological Footprint: Reducing Human Impact on the Earth.* Gabriola Island, BC: New Society Publishers, 1996.

The buildings in which these mechanical systems were applied were not effective--they were not well-insulated and had very little thermal mass. Therefore, the air conditioner or furnace had to come on fairly often, with an accompaniment of noise and a blast of dry air, to bring things back to the "balance point." The reality of this type of temperature control is like that shown on the right side of Illustration A-8. This situation is uncomfortable and unhealthy in spite of the goal of an "ideal balance."

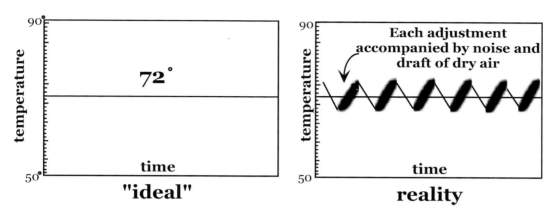

Illustration A-8 -- Ideal versus reality with regard to temperature balance

Early attempts to provide natural conditioning of buildings with passive solar architecture ran counter to the ideal of "static balance" which had become enshrined in the building codes and dictated that a building must maintain a constant temperature. In contrast, passive solar buildings maintained temperatures that dance chaotically within prescribed limits of comfort. Fortunately, the work of renowned indoor environmentalist P.O. Fanger recognized the existence of a comfort zone that was used in the eventual acceptance of passive solar buildings. The chaotic variations inherent in passive solar buildings, if designed properly, fit within the prescribed limits of Fanger's comfort zone as shown in Illustration A-9.

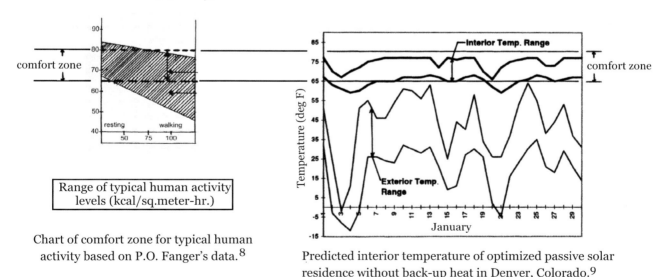

Chart of comfort zone for typical human activity based on P.O. Fanger's data.[8]

Predicted interior temperature of optimized passive solar residence without back-up heat in Denver, Colorado.[9]

Illustration A-9 -- Fanger's comfort zone and the chaotic dance of a passive solar building

8 P.O. Fanger, *Thermal Comfort:Analysis and Applications in Environmental Engineering,* McGraw-Hill, 1972.

9 Ken Haggard, Polly Cooper and Jennifer Rennick, "Natural Air Conditioning of Buildings" in *Alternative Construction: Contemporary Natural Building Methods.* Lynne Elizabeth and Cassandra Adams, Eds. Hoboken, NJ: John Wiley and Sons, 2000.

In summary, we have examples of two different concepts of thermal comfort. The first is disconnected from the natural environment and based on an "ideal balance" or constant air temperature. This approach requires high maintenance and is expensive for both humans and the planet. In contrast, natural conditioning via passive solar buildings is a comfort system connected to the environment in which chaotic temperature swings occur within the limits of the comfort zone. With this system, we rely on mechanical systems only when the temperature strays beyond the comfort zone. With natural conditioning operating costs, maintenance requirements and the impact on the planet are lessened. **This example illustrates that although the idea of balance seems very simple, it is in fact complex and challenging.**

Another trap in the quest for balance is the political use of the term. We have all seen various applications of this problem. In local land use politics, developers plead for the balance of economy and environment—arguing that economic concerns should not be too diluted by environmental concerns. In turn, environmentalists also plead for balance of the environment and economy—contending that environmental concerns should not be too diluted by economic concerns. Both are arguing from the passing industrial-era viewpoint which assumes the two are disconnected entities in opposition to each other. Our emerging sustainable era would start from the premise that the environment and economy are interconnected aspects of a larger whole that must be optimized when making decisions regarding each of these essential parts. **Therefore, balance is not about placating opposing needs, but optimizing wholes.** In this case, optimization is a better word than balance because it implies a win-win situation rather than a "balanced compromise."

Wackernagel and Rees' *Ecological Footprint* is a valuable analytical tool for critiquing the industrial society, but it will be even more valuable when it becomes an optimization tool for evaluating sustainable design decisions (see page 127). The achievement of balance in a sustainable era is more like the balance of a bicycle rider continually adjusting to multiple variations such as road shape, slope, roughness, and direction—the balance of dancing with chaos.

Beyond industrial-era thinking. Our place in nature and the question of balance are two of the most common concepts that contain unhelpful holdovers from the passing industrial era. To get beyond them we need to make mental shifts beyond the unspoken biases of industrialization. This is extraordinarily difficult because many things we take for granted could be quite the opposite in the new era. This means we can take nothing for granted—we have to approach the issue of sustainability with new minds.

To start this process we need to broaden our method of analysis. The scientific method assumes that truth can be discovered by a very careful analysis of the parts of a whole. This has been a powerful and influential mental process, but as with all things, it has limits. A contrasting approach is to perceive a situation from the perspective of integrated wholeness. This new approach will likely become just as automatic in a sustainable culture as the reductionist approach is today. Wholeness must be given importance in itself, rather than being merely something to disassemble. With regard to decision-making, this involves looking at a whole spectrum of choices before an analysis of parts begins. One mental device in this context is to view things in terms of a spectrum of possibilities rather than simple either/or choices. This approach fixes the extreme ends and makes it easier to sort out the many possibilities in between. Since we've been culturally conditioned to either/or thinking, this is a helpful analytical strategy to make the transition to evaluating multiple choices in the context of wholes.

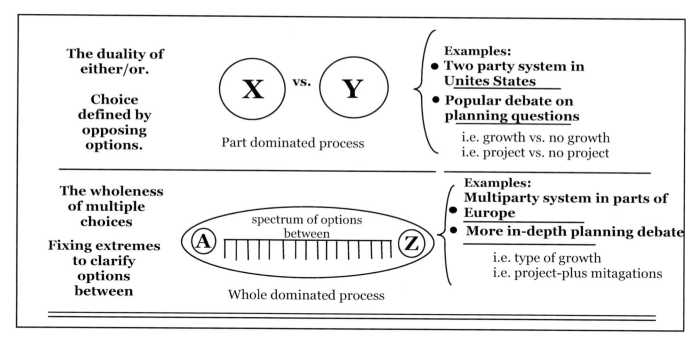

Illustration A-10 -- Two Methods of Clarifying Choices

The question regarding use of resources. The fourth basic question regarding sustainability gives us a chance to illustrate this more holistic process of analysis. Most people's first reaction to the idea of sustainability is that to be sustainable and have a smaller impact on the earth, we have to do less with less. Let's put this question into a spectrum format rather than a simple either/or question in which duality dominates and righteousness can lurk. One end of the spectrum is doing less with less. A whole social movement--voluntary simplicity--exists with this end in mind. Although voluntary simplicity is a worthwhile effort, what about the other end of the spectrum--more with more? Is that unsustainable, something to avoid totally? Let's look at these as extremes and the options between them. The idea of scarcity is such an integral part of the industrial society that it is hard to imagine not having to give up a lot of things if we move to a more sustainable culture. Is that necessarily true? Is the industrial culture most efficient at producing wealth? There is significant evidence that sustainable cultures would be more efficient in this regard.

For example: Bill Mollison, the developer of *permaculture,*[10] a man of many outrageous but thoughtful opinions, says that with permaculture techniques everyone on earth can be fed well using less than 10% of the present arable land--with the remainder restored to natural landscapes.[11] Here is one the leaders of the sustainability movement saying scarcity is not the issue; that more abundance can be created using less land and with less planetary impact through utilizing sustainable agriculture techniques.[12] This method of thinking suggests that scarcity is more a cultural state of mind than a fixed reality, and doing more with less **is** possible. It is also possible to do more with more as discussed next.

Design and technology for creating more sustainable buildings have made great progress during the last twenty years. One of these advancements is to construct buildings with straw bales. Why straw bales?

[10] *Permaculture,* or permanent culture, is a system of ecological design that works to learn from and enhance natural systems in agriculture and human settlement patterns.

[11] For more information on permaculture, visit the website: *www.permacultureactivist.net*

[12] Bill Mollison, *Permaculture: A Designer's Manual,* Tagari Publications, 1988.

A byproduct of industrialized grain farming is an overabundance of straw. This straw, particularly rice straw, is very tough and hard to compost and is considered a troublesome waste product. Farmers have been disposing of rice straw by burning it, but this produces prodigious amounts of air pollution every year and adds to the greenhouse effect by releasing large amounts of carbon dioxide into the atmosphere. But the very properties that make this material troublesome to recycle make it a superior building material. By constructing buildings of rice straw, we can do more with this particular form of agriculture and its byproducts.

Straw bale construction produces a better building while simultaneously reducing environmental impact on the planet. Pollution isn't produced from burning and carbon is sequestered in our buildings. In addition, we reduce the pressure on forests which in turn sequester carbon, clean air, create healthy watersheds and are beautiful environments and habitats. Straw bale buildings are quieter, healthier and have better insulation qualities. They are also more fireproof than standard wood-frame construction. However, there is still more that can be done with this sustainable approach to building if we continue look at the building as an integrated whole. Straw bale construction must be sealed. This is usually done by stuccoing the bale walls both inside and out. In many climates the stucco on the interior plus an exposed slab floor is about the right amount of thermal mass that the building needs to act as a passive solar building. A passive solar building is one properly oriented and tuned to heat and cool itself using sun, shade and mass. Therefore, with this technology, we are again doing more with very little increased effort or cost. Straw bale buildings provide greater comfort to the occupants at less cost to the owner and to the planet since the environmental cost of imported energy to operate the building can also be largely eliminated.

In summary, straw bale construction creates much better than standard housing while simultaneously reducing planetary impacts. The key to this process is to look at the dwelling as an integrated whole containing synergistic parts. Synergy means that the whole is more than the sum of its parts. (See page 28 for more information of synergy as an aesthetic element.) By looking at the building from a sustainable viewpoint, we achieve multiple "mores." This simple example explains why Mollison can say what seems so outrageous about agricultural productivity. He is operating from the viewpoint of integrated wholeness based on synergy rather than a system in which one aspect is stressed and other concerns put aside in the name of industrial "efficiency."

<u>Examples of straw bale buildings</u>

Illustration A-11 -- Examples of Straw Bale Buildings

A. 1. Sustainability
c. Process implications—language for a sustainable era

Language is an evolutionary system of symbols, continually changing to reflect the basic truths and biases considered important by a culture. This is why it is extraordinarily difficult to use the language of a passing cultural era to try to define a new cultural era. Illustration A-12 (page 22) shows how some of the basic processes of the industrial society and those of a sustainable society differ by comparing the language used to represent each one's beliefs.

Efficiency is at the very heart of the industrial era. It is a basic goal that drives production of goods and services. The application of this narrow view of efficiency often produces inefficient results. This is especially true regarding health. Transitioning from an industrial to a sustainable culture, as shown on the right side of the diagram, we shift the goal from maximizing efficiency to maximizing health. This shift produces opposing attitudes in our thinking about production processes, as shown by contrasting items 1, 2, 3 and 4. This shift in the meaning of efficiency has broad implications. In terms of the evolution of language, two less common words are likely to become a large part of a sustainable era vocabulary. These are *miniaturization* and *optimization*.

Miniaturization means reducing the scale of a process while simultaneously improving its efficiency. The tools and techniques of the passing industrial culture increasingly allow miniaturization to occur. Ironically, the natural evolution of industrialization is for miniaturization to replace older industrial processes which once were touted for their "efficiencies of large scale." In hindsight, these processes were heavy-handed regarding the health of the individual, society and the planet. Some of the examples shown on the lower right of Illustration A-12 are strikingly clear. These are some of the first applications of miniaturization, and will eventually convert the industrial era of "efficiency of scale" to a healthier sustainable era of "efficiency via miniaturization." Besides the information processing and energy production shown in these examples, settlement patterns and architecture are also capable of miniaturization. (See B.1., page 100, Bali as a prototype sustainable culture.)

Optimization is more than just the efficiency of a part of the whole. It means that pieces or parts can be arranged in such a way that the whole operates at its best. This is important because from the viewpoint of wholes rather than parts, the industrial society has massive inefficiencies due to disconnection between its parts. A good example is the energy economy. The Achilles heel of energy efficiency in the industrial society is the use side of the production/consumption cycle.[13] Use has become so disconnected from production in the minds of consumers that incredible wastefulness occurs because consumers are unaware of the pollution generated at far-away sites and hidden subsidies in the system. In spite of the industrial theory of "efficiencies of scale," we end up producing "inefficiencies of large scale." A simple example can be seen all around us every day—the burning of electric lights during daylight hours. Most of this serves no purpose and wastes immense amounts of expensive energy. It also adds to massive pollution loads from nuclear or fossil fuel and increases general infrastructure costs. The fact that so few of us even notice this situation is illustrative of how pervasive this social dysfunction has become. The miniaturization processes described in Illustration A-12 are the beginnings of the optimization of human activities. The result will be greater economic, environmental and social health in a sustainable era of cultural development.

---

[13] Amory Lovins, *Soft Energy Paths: Towards a Durable Peace.* New York: Harper Collins, 1979. This groundbreaking book demonstrated that efficiency cannot be measured solely by production (hard path), but also must take into account use (soft path).

PASSING INDUSTRIAL CULTURE		EVOLVING SUSTAINABLE CULTURE

GOAL: maximize efficiency
"effective operation with a
minimum of waste and effort"

Thus is a classic industrial culture we:

GOAL: maximize health
"state of being hale, sound, or whole"
"well being"

To evolve a sustainable culture we:

Passing Industrial Culture		Evolving Sustainable Culture
Look for parts	**1.**	Look for wholes
Simplify the parts	**2.**	Reintegrate wholes and parts
Disconnect from extern-alities, especially in regard to waste.	**3.**	Consider externalities; waste is seen as a resource.
Make process as large as possible to achieve economies of scale.	**4.**	Make processes as small as possible to reduce undesirable side effects while increasing efficiency by miniaturization.

WHICH RESULTS IN:

Passing Industrial Culture		Evolving Sustainable Culture
Creation of monocultures	**5.**	Creation of polycultures
Wealth at the expense of health	**6.**	Wealth and health are part of a diverse whole that can be optimized
Economy of large scale	**7.**	Economy of *miniaturization* "a representation on a much reduced scale;" smaller but still complete unto itself.

SUCCESSFUL RECENT MINIATURIZATIONS

a. Main frame computers attached to large institutions **to** personal computers at home **to** laptops anywhere **to** palm in pocket

b. Written code to run early IBM pc's **to** iconic code of early Apples

c. Buildings attached to large scale energy production systems **to** Passive solar buildings using on-site energies

d. The national energy grid **to** photovoltaic electric systems as part of the architecture on site

8. Human activity and natural processes are integrated parts of a much more optimized whole defined by health.

Illustration A-12 -- Cultural comparison of the definition of efficiency
All quotes from *Webster's International Dictionary*, 2001.

A.1. Sustainability
d. Aesthetics

Introduction. Aesthetics theory and applications are as varied as human cultures, and yet employ enough universal compositional devices that it can be understood in spite of vast differences in time, place and cultural traditions. Hence, if we are aware of the basics of composition and open enough, we can perceive with ease a variety of concerns, such as:

- the flow of the Tao in Chinese gardens
- the cosmic detachment in a Zen garden
- the rich sense of unity in a Persian mosque
- the omnipresent power and glory of the Deity in French cathedrals
- the wild exuberance of multiple gods in Balinese temples
- the terror of Aztec cosmology in building ruins in Tenochtitlan

To construct environments of this magnitude and sophistication, these expressions must be an integral part of a larger culture, even more so than individually achieved compositions such as painting, sculpture, music and dance.

Philosophers have wrestled with the question of aesthetics for a long time. Western philosophical constructions about aesthetics tend to fall between two poles, expressed here through the ideas of Plato and Tolstoy, described below in the briefest of summaries:

Plato: Aesthetics is a mere imitation of perfection that can only exist in the mind. Therefore, artists are doomed to frustration and anguish. Ideally, the most fit to rule are philosophers, because thinking, not art, is the highest human activity.

Tolstoy: Aesthetics is a heartfelt social celebration, such as found in a peasant wedding. Cultural participation is the key and the source of joy on the part of the artist who is honestly involved and connected. Art is not an artifact, but honest emotion.

To add more complexity to the realm of aesthetics is the proposition that all aesthetic movements have a birth, life and death. Historically, art and artifacts can be analyzed with regard to their place in a lifespan of this movement. One who knows the language of aesthetics and some history can approximately date objects in that context. The death of old movements and the birth of new ones are thus related to one another by the dynamics of time as well as changes in philosophy.

Architecturally, we are at just such a pregnant point today. Modern (industrial) architecture has run out of élan and is conceptually spent. "Postmodernism," defined by architects,[14] has fizzled due to its own reactionary basis, illustrating that new movements must have a certain creative force beyond just reaction to a previous movement. Presently, sustainable design is in the formative stages, and will help shape an aesthetic movement that can give impetus, experiential substance and flavor to the cultural evolution to a sustainable society—hence the emphasis on aesthetics in this book. Our discussion about aesthetics will be done in an iterative fashion. In this section aesthetics is introduced with regard to its basic structure and the implications for sustainability. On page 73 this will be discussed with regard to fractal geometry, on page 89 in relation to time, and on page 111 in relation to place.

---

[14] Postmodernism as an architectural theory is only superficially related to the post-modern movement in philosophy and literature.

Basics. Before examining what the aesthetics of sustainable design imply, it is helpful to review some fundamental elements of design aesthetics that will form the basis for discussion. Three basic design elements that are helpful in this regard are harmony, proportion and scale. By applying these elements to space, volume, function, structure and material, we can construct compositions that have certain characteristics of sequence, rhythm, order and form. If we are successful, we have created a composition containing feeling, theme and clarity. If the gods smile on us, a composition results in a whole transcending the parts.

1. Harmony. Harmony is a sense of equilibrium achieved by the compositional balance of various elements. These elements can be spaces, volumes, entrances and openings, different materials, colors, etc. Symmetry, especially bilateral symmetry, is the most obvious way of achieving harmonious balance, especially considering that humans are composed somewhat the same way (see the examples on the next page). A more intricate balance can be achieved through asymmetry, where each side of center is different but still maintains equilibrium through the mass and arrangement of its parts. Harmony can be achieved through either means. Architectural complexity allows for the opportunity to mix these devices and permits the play of contrasting elements by using both symmetrical and asymmetrical compositions. Some amazing examples exist. One of the more interesting is the example shown in Illustration A-13.

Many of the cathedrals of northern Europe utilize a strict bilateral symmetry on the entrance façade. One of the most famous, Chartres, makes a very interesting break from this bilateral symmetry. By the time the left tower was rebuilt after a fire, the technology of building cathedrals had advanced, taking stonework to a level of development not exceeded to this day. The builders had a dilemma: retain the outdated technology to maintain symmetry or use the newer refined and more daring techniques. They went for it, and the resulting building demonstrates a break in bilateral symmetry, and in the process, the creation of a building that is more expressive of a living organic process.

Illustration A-13 -- Chartres Cathedral
Central France, 1200 AD

There is also dynamic balance where one may purposefully introduce imbalance to enhance sequence or movement. This more complex sense of harmony is illustrated below.

The façade of a temple in Khajuraho, India, visually creates vibrating repetition almost like geological strata, appropriate to one of the world's oldest religions. It creates a rich asymmetrical harmony, while contrasting vertical and horizontal elements.

Illustration A-14 -- Hindu temple at Khajuraho, India (c. 1000 A.D.)

square proportion

1.61

1

1

1.61

1.61 = 1
proportion of
golden rectangle

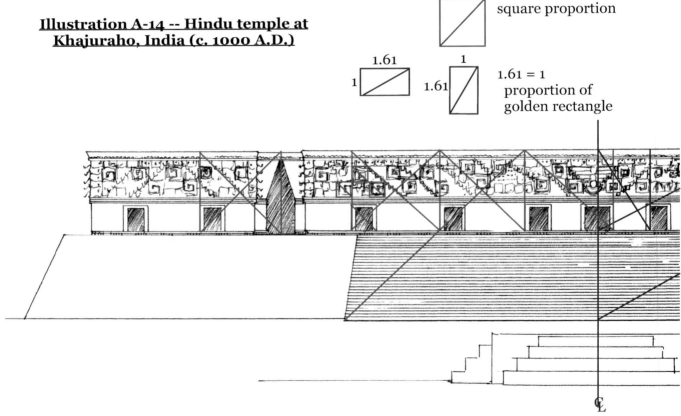

2. Proportion. Proportion is the harmonious relationship of parts to each other and to a perceived whole. In spite of the commonly held belief that "beauty is in the eye of the beholder," there are basic rules about proportion, and the application of these rules can be seen throughout history. By nature we are visually oriented animals, and therefore have a built-in proportional measuring capability integral to our senses--whether we choose to exercise this capability or not. Comparing common buildings from the turn of the century to those of the 1960s and 1970s illustrates how different design periods have exercised this capability more than others. The older buildings are almost always better proportioned. The most common mistake a designer can make is to incorporate too many elements into the composition which are not proportionally related to each other. By considering examples that are particularly successful, we can see how only a few elements can be proportionally woven into a synergistic whole, and that these relationships can be historically traced in cultures unrelated to one other, as shown below.

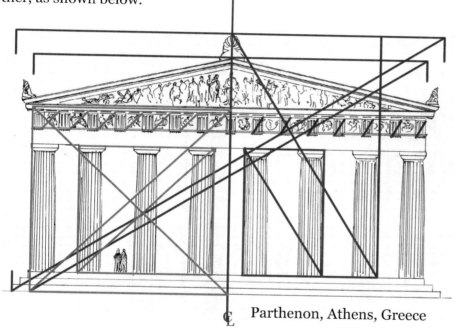

Parthenon, Athens, Greece

The composition of the front façade of the Parthenon (c. 400 B.C.) in Athens consists of the interplay of two proportions, a square shown here in red on the left side and golden rectangles (1 to 1.61) shown on the right side. Note that the columns are closer at the outer edges to visually strengthen the corners of building. The dominant proportion is the golden rectangle (shown in green in the illustration) with the emphasis on the vertical.

The composition of the façade of the Governor's Palace (c. 800 A.D.), a Mayan building, consists of the interplay of the same two proportions. The square is shown here on the left side and the golden rectangles are shown on the right. Notice that the end doorways are closer to the edge to strengthen the corners of the building. The dominant proportion is the square (shown in red in the illustration) with the emphasis on the horizontal.

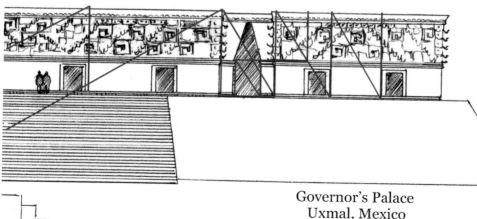

Governor's Palace
Uxmal, Mexico

Illustration A-15 -- System of proportions of two classic building façades at the same scale

26

3. **Scale.** Scale deals with the relative size of things. This may be with regard to a measuring system or the relative size of parts to a whole. An extreme case is a classical Greek temple that has an elaborate system of relating parts to the whole, but is not concerned with scale beyond itself. Temples can be monumental or diminutive but it would be impossible to tell their relative size unless people are standing near them. Unlike this example, another way to conceive of scale is in relationship to the size of a person, which we call human scale. Most vernacular architecture, residential architecture, and even some monumental architecture can achieve human scale by employing a hierarchy of elements that allows the human body to become part of the resulting composition. A third way designers have attempted to apply scale is with regard to the divine. Divine scale in a Gothic cathedral, for example, integrates space, light, material and color in a way that conceptualizes space above and beyond human scale. There is also the related concept of celestial scale. Much historical architecture such as pre-Columbian ceremonial complexes in the Americas, Egyptian and Mesopotamian architecture, and the megalithic architecture of northern Europe was based on this approach. Celestial scale employs primary elements that relate to solar, lunar and star orientation and movement. All of these are Euclidean approaches to scale. The fractal approach to scale, as we discuss in Section 2, page 63, is somewhat different. In fractal geometry there are always multiple scales from large to small that are all connected.

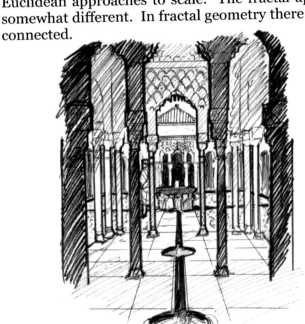

Human Scale

Divine Scale

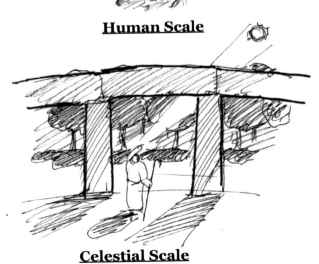

Celestial Scale

Scaleless

Illustration A-16 -- Different Approaches to Scale

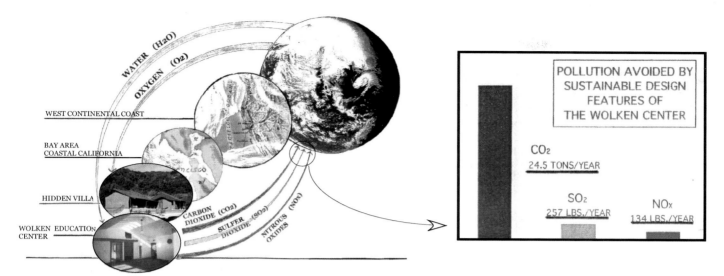

Illustration A-17 -- Fractal scale for a building in California illustrating flows

From these three basic elements--harmony, proportion and scale--we can build compositions that deal with communication, feelings and even poetry by employing the following additional elements of aesthetics:

4. **Sequence.** The movement of things.
5. **Rhythm.** The repetitious movement of things.
6. **Order.** The constructive nature of things.
7. **Form.** The shape of things.

If we achieve a successful composition utilizing all of these elements, we can convey:

8. **Theme.** The primary story told by the composition.
9. **Feeling.** The emotion conveyed by the composition.
10. **Clarity.** The clear communication of any or all of the above.
11. **Synergy.** Synergy occurs when all the elements are so well composed that the whole exceeds the sum of its parts. If really successful there is a transcendent quality to the work, a quality achieved by all great architecture and of which there are innumerable examples throughout history.

All the basic elements of aesthetics we have thus far discussed can be joined to create successful compositions. Yet, there are some pitfalls a designer must be aware of:

1. **The cliché**. The composition uses aesthetic devices that are too obvious, have been used so often as to become trite, or are too dated in the historical life of the aesthetic movement represented.
2. **The tour de force.** Literally "tower of force." The composition gives too much emphasis to some quality for its own sake--too much importance on one element at the expense of the whole. It is self-conscious or forced.
3. **The ersatz work.** The composition is trying too hard to be what it is not. It is dishonest or fake.
4. **The inappropriate work.** Through ignorance or arrogance (most arrogance is a cover for ignorance) the design doesn't fit the context, site or situation.
5. **The unresolved work.** The composition is not worked out or effort has not been taken to compose it completely; therefore, it is just plain ugly.

In regard to aesthetic movements of the recent past, "the unresolved work," was fairly common in Modern (industrial) architecture, where it was too often excused as functionalism. "The ersatz work," was fairly common to Post-Modernism, where it was excused as metaphor. As the lifespan of these aesthetic movements ran their course, more and more of the later examples resulted in "the cliché," and "the tour de force." As a result, far too much of the built environment of the past hundred years ends up as "the inappropriate work."

To illustrate this review of basics, let's examine a simple historical building type—the classical Greek temple (like the example on page 26). Here we have a forthright example of order based on Euclidean geometry, often sitting on a high site like a big piece of furniture in contrast to its surroundings. We also have a building whose classical form is not a natural result of the material with which it is constructed. What the builders did over several hundred years was to develop wood building forms and then transfer the forms to marble, resulting in a building requiring less maintenance and having more permanence. Thus Greek temples have a certain dishonesty in the relationship of form to material. So, if essentially dishonest in this regard, why are these buildings so well-regarded? Perhaps it is because they transcended their limitations by the degree of refinement they were able to express with regard to other aspects, such as relation to light, harmony and proportions. The volumetric forms utilized were an extremely good counterpart to the Mediterranean light of their setting. The mix of crisp, straight lines, sensuously curved volumes and applied sculpture is elegantly articulated by the direct light, shade and shadow that the climate allowed.

Beyond form and light, an exemplary refinement was shown in the proportions of the building. It is little wonder that the same culture developed numerical theories of proportion applied to music and drama as well as architecture. This concern for proportions became so sophisticated that Greek designers even experimented with correcting weakness in our human perceptual systems. For example, a long straight plinth (i.e. a temple base), if perfectly straight and level, will appear slightly curved to our eye (⌣). Because of this, in designing these buildings Greek architects purposefully curved the plinth in the opposite direction (⌢) to make it appear straight. This is one of the many perceptual refinements employed in these buildings for proportion and harmony to convey messages with feeling, strong theme and utmost clarity.

These messages dealt with the idea of the "golden mean"—a Greek term for the personal and social goals of balancing reason and emotion, intellect and sensuality, and that are, not surprisingly, common themes in the literature, philosophy and religion of the same period (i.e. Apollo—the cool, rational god, and Dionysus—the passionate, sensual god).[15]

Thus the classical Greek temple example turns out to be not so simple. The temple has transcended our original perception about setting and materials to speak about the universal human condition. As such, it has enough power to keep reappearing in history: in Roman architecture, Renaissance architecture, European neo-classical architecture of the 18th century, eclectic architecture of the 19th century and even occasionally in Post-Modern architecture of the late 20th century. However, each reapplication had a little less of the original spirit—a lesson about the relationship between creative integrity and aesthetic vitality.

Aesthetics of sustainability. What should be the basis of the aesthetics of sustainable design? Such a stance would incorporate the basic elements of proportion, balance and scale, and aim for synergy and transcendence. The difference would be in the areas of feeling, theme and clarity. The key to this question is in how clearly we express feeling and themes that are focused on life.

The Modernist movement inherited the scientific construct of the 17th-19th centuries that defined the universe in mechanistic and reductionist terms. The French mathematician Descartes most explicitly codified this philosophy in the 17th century.[16]

---

[15] Ruth Benedict, *Patterns of Culture*. Boston: Houghton Mifflin, 1989.
[16] Rene Descartes, *A Discourse on Method, and the Meditations*. Buffalo: Prometheus Books, 1989.

In the early polemic days of Modern architecture, Le Corbusier labeled his urbanist theories as Cartesian—architecture that would create a city based on rational, mechanically determined, highly differentiated architectural units. Following this lead thirty years later our corporate-dominated culture embraced Modern architecture. This narrow perspective created buildings dominated by short-term market considerations and mechanical climate control, all made possible by cheap, non-renewable fossil fuels. These simplistic criteria resulted in architecture that progressively became abstract and concept-dominated rather than life-oriented.

The Post-Modernist response to Modernism which occurred in the late 1970s and 1980s worked with essentially the same functional elements but pasted on to them two-dimensional façades derived from historical recall and metaphor. The result was Modern architecture, packaged in the skin of literary sensibility, as if one could civilize the beast by dressing it up. This resulted in architecture that had a compositionally different façade but was still concept-dominated rather than life-oriented.

What is meant by life-oriented? We need to reassess our priorities as every movement must do at its birth. What is the most basic purpose of environmental design? Is it to express older formative but outmoded scientific theories and esoteric artistic sensibilities, or is it to serve living beings? If we want to talk bottom-line, the *only* reason to build is to serve life. We need to return to this basic concern to transcend the conceptual traps in which aesthetics have become immersed, while simultaneously updating our perspectives on science and art, which have not stood still during the last 80 years. Newer scientific concepts that are emergent[17] in character rather than reductionist, such as ecology, ethnology and complexity, allow us to understand life differently than Descartes and Le Corbusier. The resulting Big Life perspective acknowledges that life is not just individual organisms or species or cultures, it is a whole that is interconnected. Each part is a result of and affects the whole, often in surprisingly nonlinear, chaotic ways.

Our recent problems with the ozone layer and human-induced climate change illustrate these important relationships. In fact, some scientists have postulated that the surface of our planet itself acts as a living organism—this is called the Gaia Hypothesis. Whether we accept this literally or allegorically, our design decisions and aesthetic expression should be vastly different from the past. Suddenly, our collective environmental design agenda has experienced a quantum leap in importance. How do we express this in designs that are once again life-oriented using the universal elements of architectural aesthetics?

One of the ways to accomplish this is to begin to refocus on process in design. Environmental design generally fluctuates between two poles in a spectrum of emphasis. One pole is dominated by intellectual theory emphasizing composition and polemics. The other pole is dominated by concerns with process, emphasizing integration of parts or larger concerns. Industrial planning and architecture and its predecessor and ongoing competitor, eclecticism, both proceed from the conceptual order of elements. In contrast, medieval cities and their architecture (and most vernacular architecture) proceed from the evolutionary order of things. Two vividly contrasting examples are evident in Illustrations A-18 and A-19. One is LeCorbusier's Radiant City concept for Paris in the 1920s, which became a kind of manifesto of Modernist planning and architecture. The other is the medieval city of Venice, Italy.

---

[17] Robert Laughlin, *A Different Universe–Reinventing Physics from the Bottom Down*. New York: Basic Books, 2005. A review of theoretical physics based on emergence in contrast to reductionism by a Nobel Laureate in Physics.

Le Corbusier described his urban schemes as Cartesian. This is the epiphany of conceptual form.[18] In hindsight, from the many built examples of this planning and building approach world-wide, it appears too conceptual to succeed. In contrast, Venice is complex and not orderly in the Euclidean sense. Venice grew slowly in the tidal marshes that offered its inhabitants protection, eventually becoming a very successful trading empire. Over many iterations, Venetians dealt with the flow of water, the movement of soils, and the need for circulation largely by boat. Consequently, Venice evolved into a very clear example of evolutionary form.[19]

The industrial era is rapidly passing. Process, especially life-processes, will again become a dominant part of environmental design. Fractal geometry is more process-oriented than Euclidean geometry and for this reason it will be a large part of this new approach to design (see section A.2, page 55).

Illustration A-18 -- Example of conceptually dominated order

[18] Le Corbusier, *The Radiant City*. New York: Orion Press, 1967. Le Corbusier's Radiant City concepts found their most widespread applications in the 1950s and 1960s in new industrial cities in the Soviet Bloc as well as massive low income housing projects in the U.S. In Le Corbusier's defense, it must be said that most of these projects developed only the building component without much thought to the landscape, natural lighting and ventilation aspects that existed in Le Corbusier's first prototype unit in Marseilles, France.

[19] A seminal critique of this approach to urban design was made in Oscar Newman's book, *Defensible Space*, McMillian, 1973. This book contains a devastating analysis of a particular example of high rise low income housing in Saint Louis, Missouri-- the American Institute of Architects award winning Pruitt-Igo project. Because its occupants were so deterritorialized, Pruitt-Igo became a social sink that it had to be dynamited by the authorities in 1972. The images of it's destruction were an integral part of the movie *Koyaanisqatsi* which is a severe but artful critique of the Industrial Society.

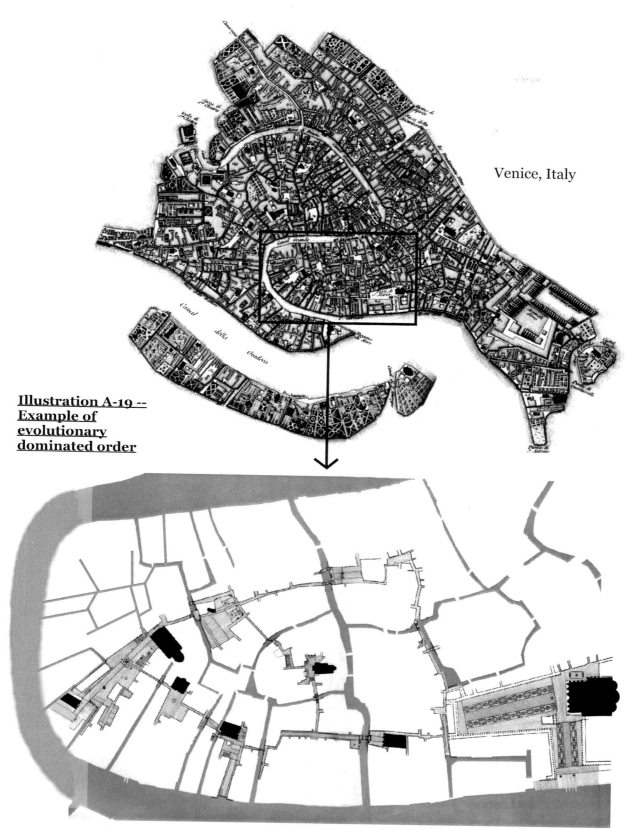

Venice, Italy

<u>Illustration A-19 --</u>
<u>Example of</u>
<u>evolutionary</u>
<u>dominated order</u>

Illustrations from Edmund Bacon, *The Design of Cities*. New York: Viking Press, 1974.

A. 1. Sustainability
e. Results

With a clear working definition, concepts of a more integrative process and a broader vocabulary regarding sustainability, we should be able to develop designs that help create and better express our evolving sustainable culture. As described in the last several pages, these designs would be concerned with the whole as much as the part, in contrast to industrial-era design. The design process would be more systematic--a system being defined "as an assembly or combination of things or parts forming a complex or unitary whole." (Webster's Dictionary 1991.)

Illustration A-21 (page 34) shows four of the most important characteristics of design in a sustainable system. Each characteristic has implications stated under "THUS," and each implication has very general guidelines or rules stated under "AND". This diagram is not meant to be read linearly. The implications and guidelines act as intersecting loops because sustainable systems are holistic.[20] They take an infinite variety of forms and applications because they are diverse. They relate to many scales because they are fractal. They dance to a chaotic rhythm because they are evolutionary. Design decisions are made over time by the process of iteration and feedback. This is the same process that generates form in fractal geometry (see page 55). Through this evolutionary process we eventually can develop high metabolic efficiencies that optimize our relationship to the unique environments we live in. Simultaneously we can create aesthetic compositions that inform us about well-being and health.

The plan for evolving the small coastal town of Los Osos, California, from a suburban bedroom community to a sustainable community is used to illustrate the application of these characteristics, implications and guidelines. This plan is shown on pages 35-48.

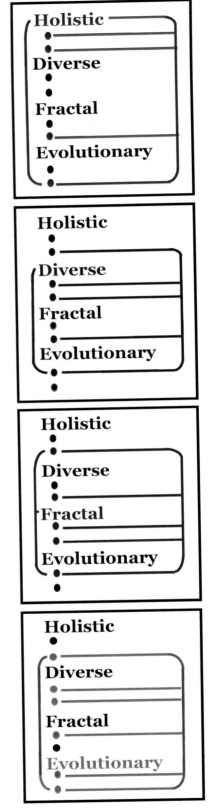

Illustration A-20 -- Interacting loops of characteristics of sustainable systems

[20] "When we try to pick any one thing out of the Universe, we find it is attached to everything else." John Muir, 1911.

Sustainable Systems are:

Holistic:

Because they consist of <u>interconnecting</u> systems at multiple scales.

THUS: All resources and energy flows are recognized to be <u>cyclic</u>.
AND: Decisions regarding sustainability are best made at the smallest scale which physically contains the system being most affected by the decision.

Diverse:

Because in ecological systems, diversity is the <u>generator</u> of health.

THUS: Decisions should enhance biological, cultural and economic diversity.
AND: Decisions at one scale should not diminish diversity at other scales.

Fractal:

Because the processes and forms involved are <u>self-similar</u> at many scales.

THUS: Decisions should enhance self-similar patterns across the widest range of scales.
AND: Aesthetics is recognized as feedback to the observer about the wholeness, diversity and health of these systems.

Evolutionary:

Because through <u>iteration</u> and <u>feedback</u>, they create diversity & efficiency.

THUS: Democracy, the political system for diversified decision making via iteration and feedback, should operate at the smallest and largest scales.
AND: Allows for the greatest efficiency when the smallest range of scale provides resources and energy flows for a particular <u>cycle</u> in this holistic entity.

<u>**Illustration A-21 -- Characteristics, implications and guidelines for sustainable systems**</u>

A. 1. Sustainability
f. Example

Section **e, Results**, stated that sustainable design involves systems that are holistic, diverse, fractal and evolutionary. This section examines the application of these characteristics to the design for the evolution of the suburban bedroom community of Los Osos, California, into a more sustainable community. This proposal, "Los Osos: A Sustainable Community within a Sustainable Watershed," was one of the first place award winners in an international competition sponsored by the American Institute of Architects and the International Union of Architects in 1993.

Introduction. The unincorporated town of Los Osos, California, population 15,500, is located along the central coast of California, twelve miles west of San Luis Obispo. It is bounded by the Pacific Ocean and a marine estuary on the west, a coastal mountain range on the south, a range of volcanic peaks to the north, and a fertile agricultural valley on the east. The eastern valley is a corridor link to San Luis Obispo, and is defined by a promenade of seven volcanic peaks. These topographic features provide this region with a unique beauty.

Los Osos lies at a crossroads in terms of future development. Without its own government, community focus or economic job base, it has grown to be a bedroom community of San Luis Obispo, a town of 60,000 people, home to the county government and a major state university. Development in Los Osos consists of largely suburban residential areas and several commercial strips that have only begun to be woven together to form a community with its own identity.

Certain aspects of design for a sustainable Los Osos are particular to its physical setting and current development concerns. This proposal examined these from the context of the four general characteristics of sustainable systems that are applicable to any community striving to function as a sustainable community.

1. HOLISTIC:
Sustainable systems are holistic because they consist of interconnecting systems at multiple scales.

With this in mind, Los Osos was examined with regard to the interconnecting systems that shape it. This was done from the broadest possible perspective, from the planetary scale down through multiple scales to the molecular level. This involves a great deal of information. A problem with urban design is how to order and make use of all the information available. The mechanism used in this case is called a "fractal scan," shown in Illustration A-22. A fractal scan is a method of looking at interconnecting systems affecting the community at a series of interesting scales or foci.

Los Osos, California
The winning design team was Polly Cooper, Marilyn Farmer, Jacob Feldman, Ken Haggard, Henry Hammer, Brian Kesner, Jora Clokey, Margot McDonald, Mark Mador, Dan Panetta, Jennifer Rennick, Randy Reynoso and Bill Whipple.

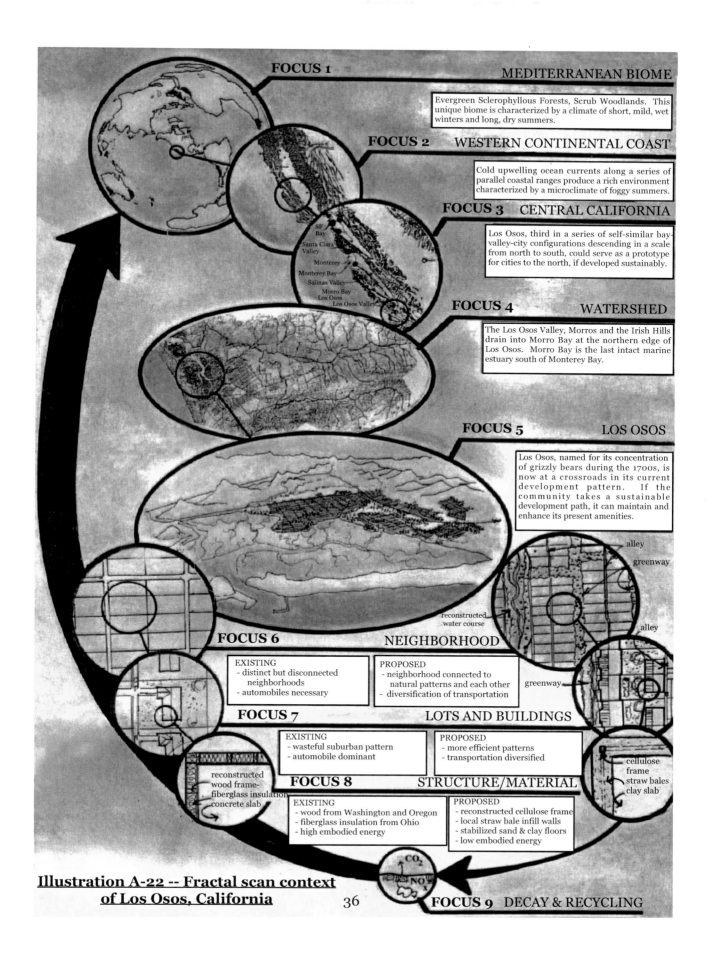

FOCUS 1 — MEDITERRANEAN BIOME

Evergreen Sclerophyllous Forests, Scrub Woodlands. This unique biome is characterized by a climate of short, mild, wet winters and long, dry summers.

FOCUS 2 — WESTERN CONTINENTAL COAST

Cold upwelling ocean currents along a series of parallel coastal ranges produce a rich environment characterized by a microclimate of foggy summers.

FOCUS 3 — CENTRAL CALIFORNIA

Los Osos, third in a series of self-similar bay-valley-city configurations descending in a scale from north to south, could serve as a prototype for cities to the north, if developed sustainably.

FOCUS 4 — WATERSHED

The Los Osos Valley, Morros and the Irish Hills drain into Morro Bay at the northern edge of Los Osos. Morro Bay is the last intact marine estuary south of Monterey Bay.

FOCUS 5 — LOS OSOS

Los Osos, named for its concentration of grizzly bears during the 1700s, is now at a crossroads in its current development pattern. If the community takes a sustainable development path, it can maintain and enhance its present amenities.

SF Bay
Santa Clara Valley
Monterey
Monterey Bay
Salinas Valley
Morro Bay
Los Osos
Los Osos Valley

alley
greenway
reconstructed water course
alley
greenway

FOCUS 6 — NEIGHBORHOOD

EXISTING
- distinct but disconnected neighborhoods
- automobiles necessary

PROPOSED
- neighborhood connected to natural patterns and each other
- diversification of transportation

FOCUS 7 — LOTS AND BUILDINGS

EXISTING
- wasteful suburban pattern
- automobile dominant

PROPOSED
- more efficient patterns
- transportation diversified

cellulose frame
straw bales
clay slab

FOCUS 8 — STRUCTURE/MATERIAL

EXISTING
- wood from Washington and Oregon
- fiberglass insulation from Ohio
- high embodied energy

PROPOSED
- reconstructed cellulose frame
- local straw bale infill walls
- stabilized sand & clay floors
- low embodied energy

reconstructed wood frame-fiberglass insulation concrete slab

CO_2
NO_x

Illustration A-22 -- Fractal scan context of Los Osos, California

36

FOCUS 9 — DECAY & RECYCLING

To look at Los Osos via a fractal scan, we focused on nine scales. The largest of these was the planetary scale, examining similar biomes to that in which Los Osos exists. This allowed clarification of the type of climate, plant communities and weather patterns that characterize a Mediterranean biome (see page 113). Next in scale was the western continental coast, which revealed geological and oceanographic conditions and the resulting microclimate: cold coastal fog in the summer and mild winters. Then attention was placed on the topographic, hydrological and geographical patterns of central California. This revealed a repetitious pattern of bays, valleys and cities: San Francisco, Monterey, and Estero Bay areas. Estero Bay, where Los Osos exists, is the southernmost, smallest and most intact of the three. The fourth focus was the watershed surrounding the town. Mapping this watershed revealed its very small size and critical importance to Los Osos. The fifth focus was the existing town and its environs. The next three foci—neighborhoods, lots and buildings, and structure and materials—were broken into two parts, the existing and proposed patterns. This allowed a comparative look at what exists and what is proposed for the design. The last focus, decay and recycling, completes the loop of this fractal scan because it deals with discharges back into the air, water and soil that reconnect back into the planetary scale. Recognizing that flows within these systems are cyclic is a major implication of holistic systems.

This scan served three functions in the sustainable design process: 1) creating a framework that gave order and aided the information gathering process, 2) digesting information into a concise graphic package directly usable in the design process, and 3) illustrating some comparable patterns with regard to existing elements and proposed elements. In this way connections between different scales can be easily visualized. This holistic perspective allowed the development of a design theme, which evolved as the regeneration of the health of the watershed of Los Osos valley. Once this theme was determined certain design decisions were relatively easy to make.

Design theme: Los Osos defined by its watershed

Viewed in the broadest context, the Mediterranean biome is fairly rare. Central California is only one of six Mediterranean biomes in the world. This biome is characterized by a climate of short, mild, wet winters with a long dry season for the remainder of the year. Its location on the western continental coast provides cold upwelling ocean currents along a series of parallel coastal mountain ranges. The Los Osos Valley watershed drains into Morro Bay at the northern edge of Los Osos, and is the last intact marine estuary, south of Monterey Bay, in northern California.

Since water is so important in this biome, the boundaries of Los Osos were defined by its watershed. One of the first design decisions was to combine the jurisdictional boundary of the city with the ecological boundary of the watershed. This was feasible because of the relatively small size of the watershed in relation to the town.

In the past, the Los Osos watershed contained native vegetation that kept the groundwater table at a high level through the dry season. This function was performed by native oak forests and marsh systems that captured the winter rains and summer fog condensation within thick vegetation and massive root systems, resulting in springs and marshes. Because oaks do not transpire much in summer heat, this reservoir provided a watershed that was wet year round. Thus, a kind of flywheel effect was provided, holding moisture for use during the long seasonal dry spells until winter rains again replenished the system. The resulting ecosystem was so rich it could support a large number of grizzly bears, for which the town was named.

While the Los Osos watershed patterns are largely intact, most of the oak forests and marshes have been destroyed in the process of development and farming. Therefore, regeneration of the riparian ecosystem became a planning priority. The basis of this design was to integrate land use with watershed restoration. Much of the fertile valley corridor within the Los Osos Valley watershed is currently utilized for agriculture, either for grazing cattle or monoculture crops. Current agricultural practices clear the land, including the riparian system and native oak trees. They are 100% dependent on fossil fuels for equipment, fertilizers and pesticides, and for the most part, export their produce. The combined effects of these practices not only destroy the health of the watershed, but also contribute to an inefficient and unstable economic base, compacted soil, erosion and toxic wastes. Watershed restoration can be achieved with new ecological farming methods that include no tillage, chemical fertilizers, pesticides or herbicides and regeneration of native oak forests. The result would be that seasonal creeks once again become perennial creeks, replenishing the aquifer and supporting a diverse ecosystem.

Transportation was another concern within the watershed that the design team considered. Plans exist to widen the road connecting Los Osos to San Luis Obispo, which would encourage even more commuting to San Luis Obispo via private automobile. In contrast, our proposal sought to reduce reliance on automobiles through a variety of approaches. These included diversifying transportation choices by providing facilities for public transit, bicycles, mopeds, electric automobiles, walking and horseback riding, and to reducing the need for automobile use by increasing Los Osos-based employment opportunities. These methods could allow for the stabilization of the traffic corridor and restoration of the drainage and riparian patterns it has disrupted (see Illustration A-31). Transportation solutions and the watershed could enhance each other rather than being in conflict.

Watershed restoration connecting riparian corridors in existing residential and commercial areas was proposed along the original drainage patterns. These corridors would not only restore the watershed and aquifers, but would also provide linkages between neighborhoods with connecting paths for pedestrians and bicycles.

Wastewater was another important concern when looking at the watershed holistically. Presently, all of Los Osos uses septic systems for wastewater treatment. Being located on old sand dunes with good water percolation allowed an unusual density of septic systems, but now this method for wastewater treatment has reached its limit. The county and state have demanded conversion to a standard sewer system, which the town is resisting.[21] As an alternative to this expensive system, the sustainable plan proposes a water treatment and recovery system composed of ponds and marshes called an Advanced Integrated Pond System (AIPS), developed by Dr. William J. Oswald (see page 50 for more details). Besides providing clean water, open space and wildlife habitat, this alternative system produces energy by methane generation and provides water and compost for gardens. It was proposed that the AIPS system be part of a new town center for Los Osos. This allowed it to function as an urban feature, making cyclic flows visible. In this location, it can enhance the town socially, economically and environmentally while costing less than a traditional sewer plant. It also provides a highly visible example that sustainable systems can provide *more* while costing less.

---

[21] The State Water Quality Control Board and San Luis Obispo county have mandated a $71.5 million sewer system for Los Osos. This has been resisted because each resident would be liable for more than $100 per month, or almost $40,000 with interest and operating costs over a thirty-year period. Failure to buy in to this sewer system has resulted in an eighteen-year building moratorium in Los Osos.

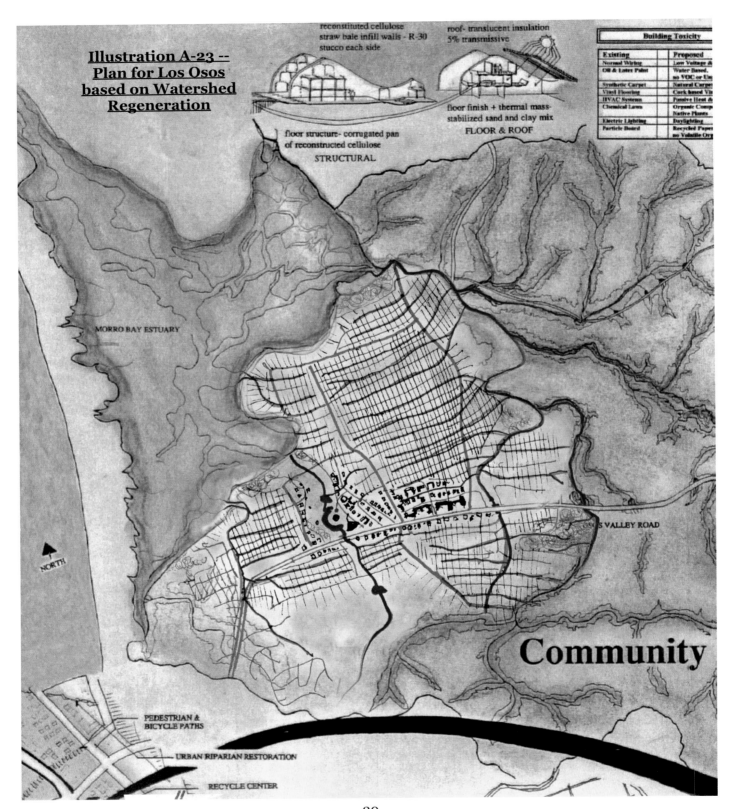

Illustration A-23 --
Plan for Los Osos
based on Watershed
Regeneration

reconstituted cellulose
straw bale infill walls - R-30
stucco each side

roof- translucent insulation
5% transmissive

floor structure- corrugated pan
of reconstructed cellulose

STRUCTURAL

floor finish + thermal mass-
stabilized sand and clay mix

FLOOR & ROOF

Building Toxicity	
Existing	Proposed
Normal Wiring	Low Voltage &
Oil & Latex Paint	Water Based, no VOC or Un
Synthetic Carpet	Natural Carpet
Vinyl Flooring	Cork based Vi
HVAC System	Passive Heat &
Chemical Lawn	Organic Comp Native Plants
Electric Lighting	Daylighting
Particle Board	Recycled Paper no Volatile Org

MORRO BAY ESTUARY

NORTH

S VALLEY ROAD

Community

PEDESTRIAN &
BICYCLE PATHS

URBAN RIPARIAN RESTORATION

RECYCLE CENTER

Building Toxicity

Relative Toxicity
60
50
40
30
20
10
0
1900 1960 1980 Proposed
Year of Construction

and vice versa, and by

3. restoring the flywheel effect through riparian restoration and progressive human water treatment.

WATERSHED RESTORATION
THE "FLYWHEEL" EFFECT

WINTER RAIN

Oaks don't transpire in the summer heat.

FOG CONDENSATION

SOIL MOISTURE
Layers of organic matter act as a sponge -once saturated will slowly release water.

SPRINGS

CAPILARY ROOT ACTION

AQUIFER RECHARGE

Deer are depend on the Oaks

RIPARIAN

Watershed Boundary and City Limits of Los Osos, CA

Defined by Watershed

0   1000   2000   5000

2. DIVERSE:

Sustainable systems are diverse because in ecological systems, diversity is the generator of health.

Development of Los Osos to date has been one of diminishing diversity. This is true with regard to landscape, watershed, housing types and transportation. Reversing this trend was a major objective of the design team. Maximizing diversity was considered essential to all aspects of this proposal. This was extended beyond current thinking most radically in the realm of housing.

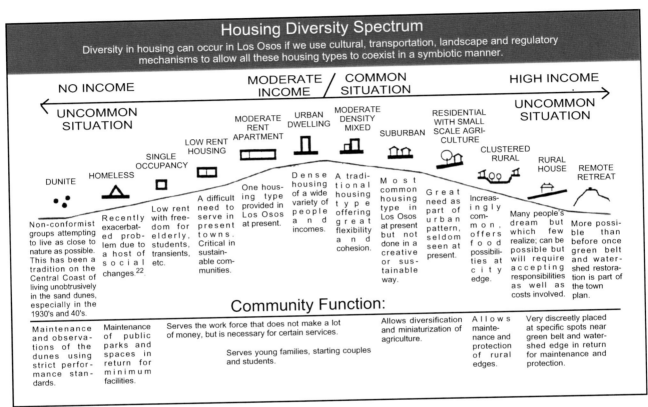

Illustration A-24 -- Housing Diversity Spectrum

The proposal first examined all the types of housing that might possibly exist in Los Osos without bias regarding desirability or practicality. These housing types were then arranged in a spectrum based on affordability, from very inexpensive to very expensive. The team found this spectrum to be a version of the classic bell curve with the most common types in the center and the least common at each end.

If we were to be serious about diversity in housing, all of these types must be provided for in the sustainability plan for Los Osos. We should not only provide them all, but they should all contribute something to the community by their uniqueness. The key was determining where in the plan each type could occur and what community function they could fulfill as part of a holistic zoning system that maximized diversity. For example, let's consider what is traditionally the least community-oriented housing type: the one we have labeled the "rural house." This is a very expensive option that often takes the form of a gated enclave completely cut off from the rest of the community.

22 For more on creative responses to homeless questions, see *The Quality of Mercy* by Paul Lee, Platonic Academy Press, on homelessness in Santa Cruz, 1983-1992, and explore the examples occurring in Portland, Oregon by the organization City Repair.

The Trout Farm Complex

OPEN-FACED MINE (CHROMIUM 1914 & 1944)

ROADS

MINING DIGS

GRADED PADS

RUINS OF ORE GRINDING MILL

OLD LEECHING PONDS NOW TROUT PONDS

PARKING LOT

STREAMS

20th century Impacts

PUBLIC PEDESTRIAN ACCESS TO NATIONAL FOREST

EROSION CONTROL AND CONVERSION OF ROAD CUTS TO PATHS

FOREST REGENERATION

EDUCATIONAL TOURS ON SUSTAINABLE BUILDING DESIGN

STREAM AND POND MAINTENANCE, AND RED-LEGGED FROG REHABILITATION

21st century Regeneration

Illustration A-25 -- Cycle of impacts and regeneration of the Trout Farm

But what if rural zoning had certain very specific responsibilities that would go along with the unique privileges of this housing type? Further, what if these responsibilities were regularly evaluated with performance standards that considered the following:

- protecting and maintaining native species of plants and animals
- protecting and enhancing threatened and endangered species
- enhancement of natural features by creative stewardship (ponds, vernal pools, etc.)
- turning old road cuts and scars into paths
- controlling erosion and maintaining creeks and drainage systems
- fire protection via prevention and controlled burns
- allowing and maintaining public right-of-way into public lands
- education and tours for public about unique cultural and ecological features

All this may sound impractical, but this innovative ecological design strategy is already taking place at the Trout Farm Complex located on the Central Coast of California (see page 138). This is a unique place that has been degraded by mining, grading, motorcycle racing and wild fires. It is now being regenerated and enhanced by human occupancy. The key is to plan for diversity and then be creative about providing and enhancing it. For those on the political right this approach is less restrictive than existing zoning where rules are strictly based on density. For those on the left it means enhancing diversity based on concern for the larger community within a holistic design system, adding responsibility to privilege.

42

Another illustration of design for diversity was developed by redesigning the most common type of housing in Los Osos, the suburban home, to fit the unique location. This example is shown in foci 6 and 7 in the existing and proposed parts of the fractal scan on page 36.

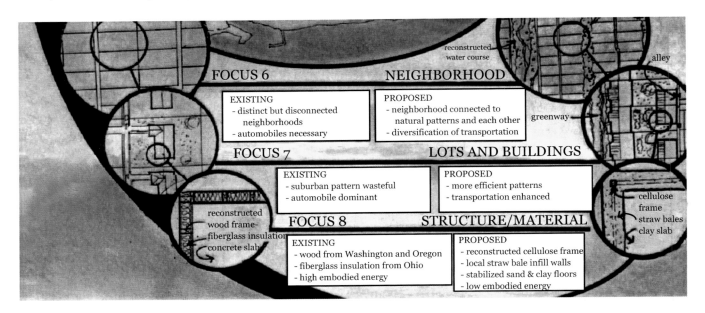

Illustration A-26 -- Modification of suburban housing pattern in Los Osos

These design modifications were based on neotraditional planning theory. However, instead of retaining a standard 19th century pattern, the design team adapted these techniques to the specific conditions of Los Osos and 21st century sustainable building technologies.

Planning principles

1. Regenerate, incorporate and celebrate the existing riparian patterns of Los Osos.
2. Use on-site energies in buildings. Housing should provide passive solar heating, natural lighting, natural ventilation and photovoltaic panel generated electricity. All buildings should be designed with optimal solar access.
3. Use local building materials as much as possible. Some building materials (e.g., straw bales) are currently waste products, yet are very good for passive solar use because they provide both superior insulation and, once stuccoed, good distributed thermal mass.
4. Mix various housing types such as small moderately priced rental units and single occupancy homes in an integrated pattern. This allows more flexibility and greater social diversity in what has traditionally been a monolithic housing zone.
5. Create more open space, more efficient interior space and optimal solar orientation while increasing density.
6. Tame the automobile and transportation infrastructure by creation of a system of alleys as used in traditional town planning in the United States.

43

Resulting plan characteristics

The riparian patterns in Los Osos are proposed as the major organizing element in the new housing pattern. These regenerated waterways were designed to be 60' wide habitat, pedestrian and play rights-of-way in the new plan.

In the design, a system of 25' wide alleys and larger streets are provided. The alleys are parallel to the riparian rights-of-way.

The lots are 100' deep by 25' wide and are located between a riparian right of way and an alley. This creates 3000 sq. ft. lots instead of the existing 6000 sq. ft. lots, doubling the density of the housing pattern.

Homes situated on these lots are sited in a modified row house pattern using straw bale party walls, which provides superior sound and fire resistance. Single-occupancy rentals, studios, elder and teen units and secondary buildings such as with garages and shops are located on the alley side to create a courtyard pattern. Therefore, at even twice the density, there is more usable open space than in a typical suburban subdivision.

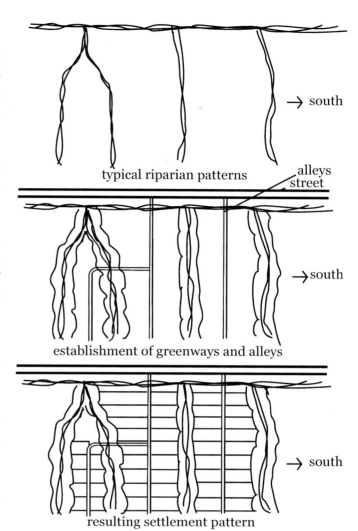

typical riparian patterns

establishment of greenways and alleys

resulting settlement pattern

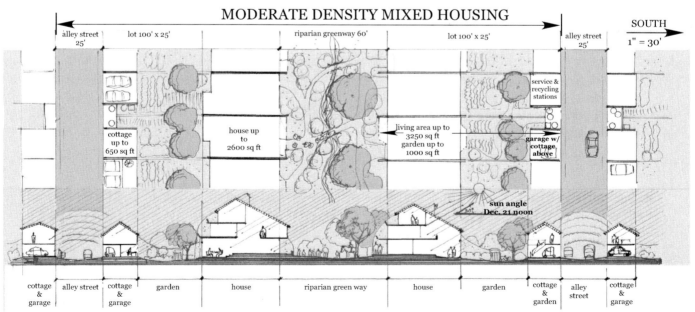

Illustration A-27 -- Resulting plan characteristics of housing integrated with watershed

44

Architectural characteristics

Between the straw bale party walls are flexible arrangements of 1-, 2- and 3-story spaces oriented to allow solar access. This arrangement allows for twice the interior floor space of a standard subdivision.

Optimized passive thermal performance is provided by direct gain through the whole roof and the distributed thermal mass of the floors and walls. Cooling loads are very small in this microclimate where some of the coolest weather occurs in the summer when coastal fogs are prevalent. Due to this situation, the whole roof can be collectors of various types. A composite roof consisting of transparent insulation and photovoltaic cells, designed to be 5% translucent, is proposed. The result is that the buildings can largely heat themselves and produce electricity. An intertie system uses the electrical grid as a back-up system. The occupant sells energy back to the energy company during peak production periods and then buys energy during cloudy or foggy periods. This system would allow Los Osos to be electrically self-sufficient, avoiding vulnerability to the fluctuating electrical supply, availability and price manipulation that has been a big problem in California.

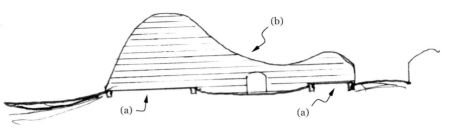

1. (a) native sand plinth with grade beams at edges. (b) load-bearing straw bale party wall (16" thick).

2. (c) light steel (recycled) frame bolted together for flexibility of future configurations, and light steel deck for floors.

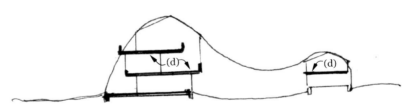

3. (d) stabilized earthen floors on light steel decks.

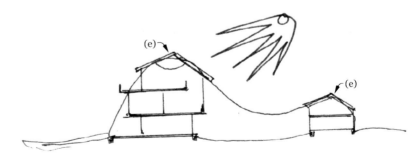

4. (e) roof membrane consisting of layers of transparent insulation and translucent photo voltaic panels arranged to optimize thermal, electrical production, and solar hot water potentials.

Illustration A-28 -- Resulting architectural characteristics

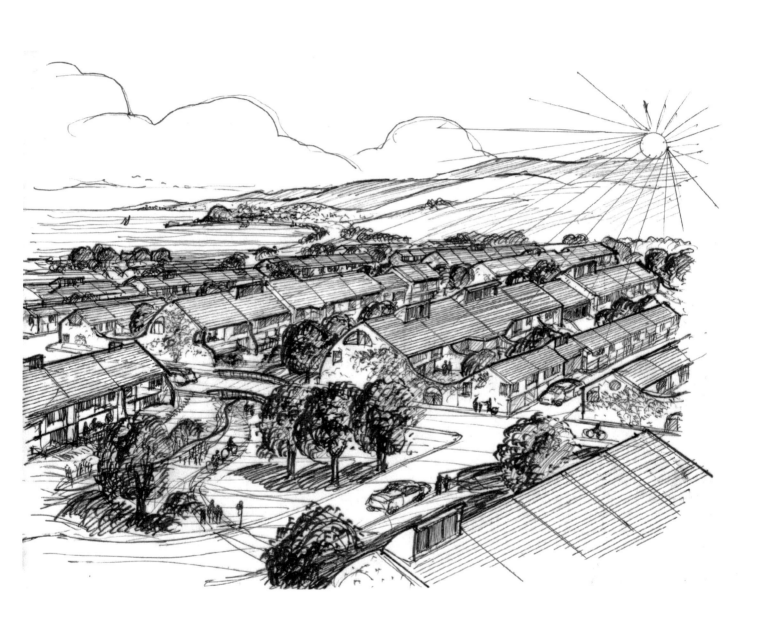

Illustration A-29 -- Housing integrated with riparian patterns

3. FRACTAL:
The processes and forms of sustainable systems are self-similar at many scales.

The multi-view of the fractal scan provided the framework necessary to develop a plan for Los Osos. Much of this framework involves fractal patterns that are the result of chaotic processes that occur in nature. As stated earlier, chaos is used here in the scientific sense of unpredictable behavior, not in the literary sense of fearful disorder. Two of the earliest recognized chaotic processes are water flow as a part of a landscape and weather as part of a climate.

The team defined Los Osos by its watershed, combining both jurisdictional and watershed boundaries. As a result, the plan, by definition, had to have fractal aspects. The branching fractal pattern of the riparian drainage system became the basic framework around which agriculture, transportation, public works and housing patterns were developed. The watershed and its many parts became a living, integral part of the town rather than something requiring linear control in engineered concrete culverts or drainage ditches.

The plan is also fractal in that each element of the system is designed with concern for sustainability and health, and for the positive effect on other elements at a series of interconnected scales.

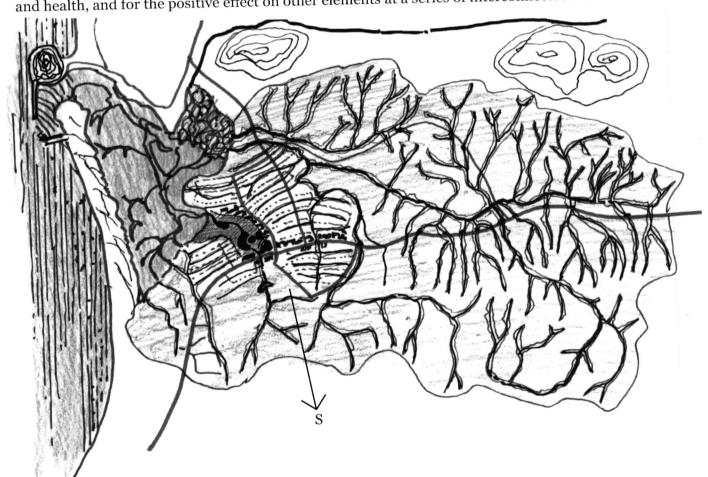

S

Illustration A-30 -- Fractal Pattern of Los Osos Riparian System

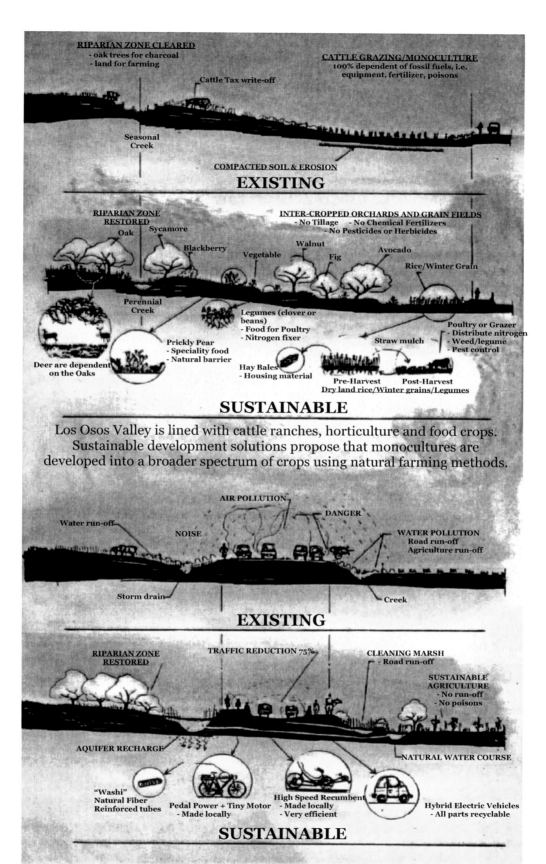

Los Osos Valley is lined with cattle ranches, horticulture and food crops. Sustainable development solutions propose that monocultures are developed into a broader spectrum of crops using natural farming methods.

Illustration A-31 -- Agriculture and transportation integrated with watershed

48

4. EVOLUTIONARY:
Through iteration and feedback, sustainable systems create diversity and efficiency.

Evolution implies modifications in a sequence of events; thus its processes are similar to the interactive-feedback process that evolves fractal forms. This is the last of the four characteristics described because it demonstrates many of the connections between all four.

Evolution, as applied to the political process, is a necessary part of physical planning and implementation. In a democracy, political decision making is largely done through elections occurring at prearranged times. Running as a candidate in an election is equivalent to iteration, and voting is equivalent to feedback. Therefore, the democratic process is iterative and evolutionary. It is also not wholly predictable, and thus chaotic, and because it occurs at a series of scales--from national to city--in a self-similar pattern, it could also be considered fractal. Making democratic decisions at the local level is more efficient and beneficial because the decisions are closer to the system in question. This is why the first step of the Los Osos plan was to merge the city limits with the watershed boundary.

Clarity is necessary for informed democratic decision-making. Voters must understand what is involved, why the issue affects them, and that they can indeed have an influence on the outcome. As a consequence it is important that the decision-making and resultant infrastructure be transparent. There must be visual clues that allow as much understanding of what is going on as possible.

A good example of this in the Los Osos plan is the wastewater treatment and recycling infrastructure. Aside from the environmental and economic advantages discussed, there is an equally important advantage of public consensus. This is facilitated by making the Advanced Integrated Pond System treatment process an integral part of the civic space at the town center on axis with the Morro Bay

Estuary and the entry to the heart of the city. In this location it is intimately connected to public buildings and other facilities rather than being isolated at the edge of town, out of sight, mind and understanding. If the wastewater plant were isolated, it would be taken for granted and fall into the dysfunctional situation where little feedback occurs. This happens frequently with modern large-scale infrastructure, such as regional electric grids, importation of water from foreign watersheds and ubiquitous highway systems. To have and maintain a sustainable and informed society the public must have intimate knowledge of the systems that make it so.

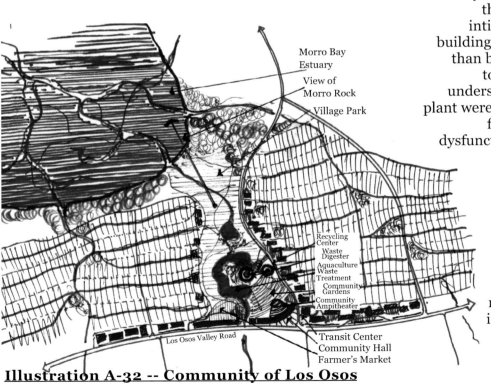

Illustration A-32 -- Community of Los Osos

New Community Focus

Los Osos, population 15,000, currently consists of three distinct neighborhoods which are bedroom communities for the city of San Luis Obispo, population 60,000, twelve miles away. Unincorporated Los Osos has no government or civic center and is fragmented by the strip commercial Los Osos Valley Road. The existing undeveloped land for the proposed new community center lies at a crossroads at the center of the three neighborhoods and thus offers the possibility of establishing a focus, model and mechanism for the evolution of a sustainable community.[23]

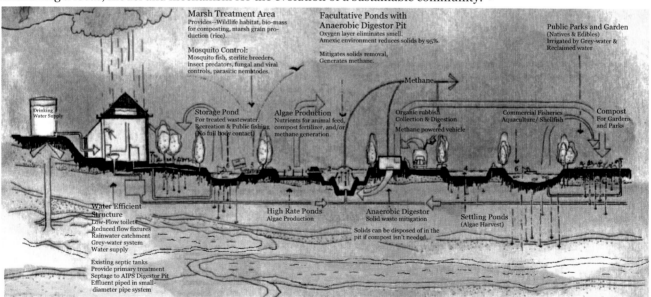

<u>Illustration A-33 -- Resource recovery and wastewater treatment as part of new community center</u>

[23] This water recovery system using treatment ponds and marshes is called Advanced Integrated Pond Systems (AIPS) and was developed by Dr. William J. Oswald. Working examples exist in Arcata, Delhi, and St. Helena, California.

General design principles of Sustainability

The urgent need to reduce destructive human impact on the planet brings new importance to sustainable design. It is through good design that the processes of miniaturization and optimization will be realized. The ability to do this, however, also requires the design professions to refine approaches and change assumptions.

One change is the way the environmental design professions are organized. Distinctions between professions are presently based on scale as much as subject. Planners envision policy and implementation on a large scale. Landscape architects deal with land, habitat and vegetation ranging from large to relatively small scales. Architects design entire complexes or single buildings. Engineers develop structures and infrastructure systems. Industrial designers deal with artifacts. The barriers between these approaches are presently too fixed and static, with not enough flow between different scales. Specialization has developed in such a way as to create dysfunction in how these different approaches affect each other. Each scale is well defined but not well connected. The definition and organization of the different design professions will have to evolve to fulfill the opportunities and responsibilities of sustainable design.

A fractal view of scale and organization will help this problem. This approach maintains the general scale definitions but recognizes that each scale contains aspects of all the others. No matter how large or small any planning or design situation is, it contains parts of all the other scales in an integral whole. We must deal with all the other scales of design at each particular scale.

Basic design assumptions taken from the industrial era will have to be examined closely. The Los Osos plan, illustrated on the previous pages, contains design decisions that are not difficult, but fly in the face of many industrial era design assumptions currently taken for granted. We need to recognize that:

Sustainable systems are holistic -- beyond merely parts.

Sustainable systems are diverse -- beyond simply single purpose.

Sustainable systems are fractal -- beyond only Euclidean.

Sustainable systems are evolutionary -- beyond status quo or revolutionary.

Sustainable systems allow fresh approaches to what now seem insurmountable problems. The remaining sections on fractal geometry, time and place will elaborate further on these design considerations.

holistic

diverse

evolutionary

fractal

52

WE ARE EMBEDDED IN AN ENVIRONMENT OF FRACTAL PATTERNS. SHOWN HERE ARE FRACTAL PATTERNS SEEN WHILE FLYING OVER SOUTHEASTERN CALIFORNIA.

THE CONCEPT OF FRACTAL GEOMETRY

A.2. Fractal Geometry
a. definitions

Introduction: Due to the degree of human specialization in the scientific/industrial era, we live in a world of thousands of dialects. This book is written in the dialect of Environmental Design, which includes Urban and Regional Planning, Architecture, Landscape Architecture, Product Design and Engineering (structural, mechanical, environmental and civil), each of which has its own sub-dialect. We are asking these fields to consider concepts from fractal geometry and sustainability. To utilize these concepts, it is not necessary for designers to learn an entirely new dialect. We will not go into a complete description of fractal geometry or great detail about the mathematics involved. Instead we hope this section--a Fractal Primer--will provide enough vocabulary on fractal geometry to allow the reader to evaluate the design proposals in the rest of this book. These proposals are an attempt to illustrate how design tools from fractal geometry and sustainability can help humankind become more attuned to our planetary opportunities and responsibilities.

This primer is structured sequentially from simple to more complex concepts. The basic assumptions of fractal geometry are developed on a progressively unfolding chart which compares them to the assumptions of Euclidean geometry. The completed chart on page 71 is a summary of this primer and forms the basis for the examples at the end of this section. The emphasis of this primer is form generation, since this is of central concern to designers. The types of form generation include:

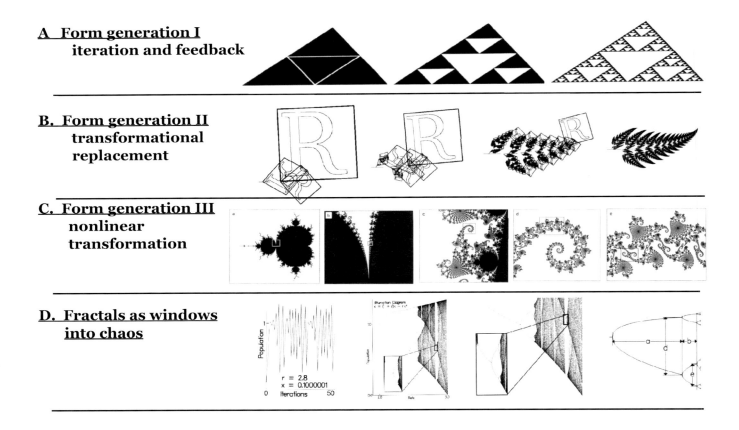

A   Form generation I
   iteration and feedback

B. Form generation II
   transformational
   replacement

C. Form generation III
   nonlinear
   transformation

D. Fractals as windows
   into chaos

What is fractal geometry? B.B. Mandelbrot, the father of fractal geometry,[24] wrote, "Broadly speaking, mathematical and natural fractals are shapes whose roughness and fragmentation neither tend to vanish or fluctuate up and down, but remain essentially unchanged as one zooms in continually and examination is refined. Hence the structure of every piece holds the key to the whole structure."[25] In the dialect of architecture and environmental design, this might be translated: In fractal geometry, forms tend to be related and repeated at any scale at which we focus our attention. Every piece of the visual or spatial composition is related to the whole and vice versa.

The concept of **continuity of scale** is one of the most useful aspects of fractal geometry. If we assume nature is a holistic, complex pattern in which we are embedded and in which we design and build, then fractal geometry can be an easier way to describe and design within our condition. Because of this, fractal geometry should become a design tool as important as Euclidean geometry. For environmental design, fractal geometry is an extension of Euclidean geometry that allows us to deal more comfortably with complex form and circumstance. In the following primer we compare one system to the other, as in the diagram below.

A.2. Fractal Geometry
b. Fractal primer

It is the things we take for granted, our unspoken assumptions, which determine our approach and affect the outcome of any design. If we unquestionably apply Euclidean geometry to the design process, we also apply its assumptions. If we have a choice in geometries, we can consider the assumptions on which each is based, allowing us to become more conscious of our decisions. Initial comparisons of the basic assumptions of Euclidean and fractal geometry are listed below. They begin to illustrate why fractal geometry is so important to environmental design for a sustainable era.

ABOUT	Basic assumptions behind Euclidean geometry (2000 years old)	Basic assumptions behind fractal geometry (20 years old)
1. **description**	The main concern is the description of human-made objects. Natural objects are assumed to be difficult to describe or indescribable by geometry	There is holistic reality, infinitely complex but geometrically describe-able, which we call nature.
2. **form**	Simple rules give simple forms. Complex forms require complex rules; therefore simplicity is a virtue.	Infinitely complex forms are easy to generate by simple means. Complexity is an integral part of reality and is accessible to us. Simplicity can be a virtue, but can also be simplistic. Complexity is our bio-logical heritage.
3. **form generation**	Formulae are the generator of form.	Iteration and feedback are the generator of form.

---

[24] There are many good references available on fractal geometry. Two that are the most accessible to designers are: *An Eye for Fractals* by Michael McGuire, Perseus Books, 1991 and *Fractal Geometry in Architecture and Design* by Carl Bovill, Birkhauser 1996. Graphics and material on pages 55, 58, 59, 60, 62, 64, 67, and 68 are taken directly from *An Eye for Fractals* and used with kind permission of the author Michael McGuire and his publisher Perseus Books.

[25] "Fractal Geometry: What is it and What Does it Do?" *Proceedings of the Royal Society*, London, May 1989.

We can see from the basic assumptions of both systems that Euclidean geometry is the traditional formal geometry of objects made by humans. Fractal geometry, in contrast, is concerned with a timeless organic geometry of natural forms and patterns. To work more closely with nature than we have in the recent past, architecture for a sustainable society must be based on fractal geometry as well as Euclidean geometry. These different ways of thinking affect such basic concepts as our definitions of what constitutes dimension, scale, order and form. Equally important are differences that concern relationships to surroundings. Because geometry is such a basic conceptual tool, it affects the way we view, interact with, and manipulate reality. Once the basis of fractal geometry is absorbed and made as much a part of our intuitive thinking as Euclidean geometry, we can never look at the environment and architecture the same way again.

Form generation I: Dimension, iteration and feedback

Euclidean geometry is based on the idea of three dimensions of three whole numbers: the one-dimensional line, the two-dimensional plane, and the three-dimensional volume. In fractal geometry, dimension is more complex. Here, dimension can be most easily defined in relation to the form-generation process.

As the chart on the previous page illustrates, form generation in fractal geometry is accomplished by repeating a process (iteration) to modify the preceding object (feedback). Let's use these processes to modify a simple one-dimensional Euclidean object, a line, into a two-dimensional Euclidean object, a plane:

Object #1	line n $n/3$ $n/3$ $n/3$	A line (one dimension) of length n consisting of equal parts $1/n$ in length (shown in this case where n=3)
Iteration #1 **Object #2**	3 2 4 1 5 9 6 8 7	use n=3 1. Replace the center line with 6 new lines and feed back into object #1 to create object #2 consisting of 9 equal pieces
Iteration #2 **Object #3**		2. Repeat this process using each line of object #2 with a second iteration and feedback to create object #3.
Iteration #3 **Object #4**		3. Repeat this process indefinitely as if we have a microscope to track successive details at a finer and finer grain. The result after only a few iterations is the modification of our original one-dimensional line to a two- dimensional plane in the Euclidean sense.

Illustration A-34 -- Form generation of a Peano curve

There is a formula for determining the fractal dimension of an object constructed by iteration and feedback.

It is: **D = log N / log n**   where:

Dimension of the object = log of the number of pieces produced at each iteration, divided by the magnification needed to get back to the original object.	**D**= dimension **N**= number of pieces at each iteration **n**= magnification needed to get back to the original object

For those not familiar with logarithms, the *Webster's Dictionary* definition is:
"Logarithm—the exponent of that power to which a fixed number, called the base unit, can be raised to provide a given number called the antilog; or: **log a^b = b log a**"

Thus, for object #1, **D = log 3 / log 3 = 1.**
For object #4 the dimension is **D = log 9 / log 3 = 2** | This agrees with Euclidean geometry where the dimension of a line is 1 and the dimension of a plane is 2.

Therefore, this system is in agreement with the Euclidean system, although object #4 is a fractal curve created from a line that has filled a two-dimensional plane by the process of iteration and feedback. Euclidean and fractal geometry aren't in conflict. Fractal geometry grows from Euclidean geometry, filling the gaps in it. The object #4 we just created was first proposed by Giuseppe Peano in 1890. It is called a Peano curve and is one of the classic fractal curves developed at the end of the 19th century. This development occurred at same time as the development of a fresh, integrated approach in the arts and architecture which also took a new look at more complex forms based on nature.[26] This occurrence seems to be more than coincidental. The period in question, the "*fin de siécle,*" may have been a preview of the potential for human development. This creativity was drastically interrupted by the return to the source of industrialized warfare which had allowed Europe and North America to dominate the world. The two great industrial wars that devastated Europe destroyed its colonial empires and ended this period of creative optimism. The fresh, new approach to design was replaced by a progressively more strident industrial expression that culminated in the Modernism of the mid-20th century. The early fractals, without computers to facilitate easy manipulation, were so upsetting to the established order that they were assigned to a gallery of "monsters," where they were set aside as mathematical oddities to be ignored until our time—the second "*fin de siécle*" and new millennium. Only now has information processing technology developed enough to allow the freeing of these "monsters."

For those bothered by using the formula for fractal dimension without explanation, here is a simple derivation:
1. Taking a line and cutting it into pieces gives us **n** number of pieces of size 1/n (1 dimensional object).................
2. Likewise, a square cut into **n** pieces in width and length gives us **n** x **n** or **n²** number of pieces of size 1/n...................................
3. Likewise, a cube cut into **n** pieces in width, length, and height gives us **n** x **n** x **n** or **n³** number of pieces of size 1/n...................
Thus, in Euclidean geometry, we can see the exponent of **n** = the dimension of the object.
Let's convert all of this into logarithms which is an easy way of keeping track of exponents.
Where **log a^b = b log n**   (by definition)
Thus, **log N = 1 log n** for a one dimensional object, **log N = 2 log n** for a two dimensional object, and **log N = 3 log n** for a three dimensional object; or **log N = D log n**.......now divide each side by **log n**
log N /log n = D   (from above **N** = number of pieces, and **n** = multiplication times to get back to the original object size).
Therefore, **D = log (number of pieces) /log (magnification factor of pieces)**

This is the equation we used to determine the fractal dimension of object #4.

---

[26] Examples include Art Nouveau (France), Arts and Crafts (Britain), Modernista (Spain), Jungenstil (Germany), Secessionist (Austria), Liberty (Italy), and Craftsman (United States).

To complete this section on form generation and dimension, let's develop some more fractal curves. The following is one developed by Helge von Koch in 1904, appropriately called the Koch curve. This simple iterative process is called line replacement by addition.

new pieces = 4
magnification factor = 3

Therefore, the fractal dimension =
log 4/ log 3 = 1.26

Illustration A-35 -- Koch curve

Performing the same interactive process on a two-dimensional plane like a triangle, we get an object called a Koch snowflake, the result of object replacement by addition.

 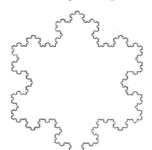

new pieces = 12
magnification factor = 3

Therefore, the fractal dimension =
log 12/ log 3 = 2.4

Illustration A-36 -- Koch snowflake

What's going on here? Can dimension be fractional and not a whole number? In fractal geometry, the answer is yes. This is why, in fractal geometry, there are an infinite number of dimensions that can exist between the whole-numbered dimensions of Euclidean geometry, just as the Koch curve exists between one and two dimensions and the Koch snowflake between two and three dimensions.

Fractals can also be created by subtracting pieces rather than adding them. This is called line replacement by subtraction. Below is an example where we remove the center third of a line in a series of iterations and feedback. The result is a pattern called Cantor dust after the mathematician George Cantor who developed this fractal in 1883.

new pieces = 2
magnification factor = 3

Therefore, the fractal dimension =
log 2/ log 3= .63

Illustration A-37 -- Cantor Dust

Another fractal developed by subtraction is the Sierpinski gasket by Waclaw Sierpinski in 1919. In this case, we remove the center of a triangular plane with each iteration, an object replacement by subtraction process. We would expect the fractal dimension of the result to be between one and two dimensions since we're infinitely punching out parts of a two dimensional plane.

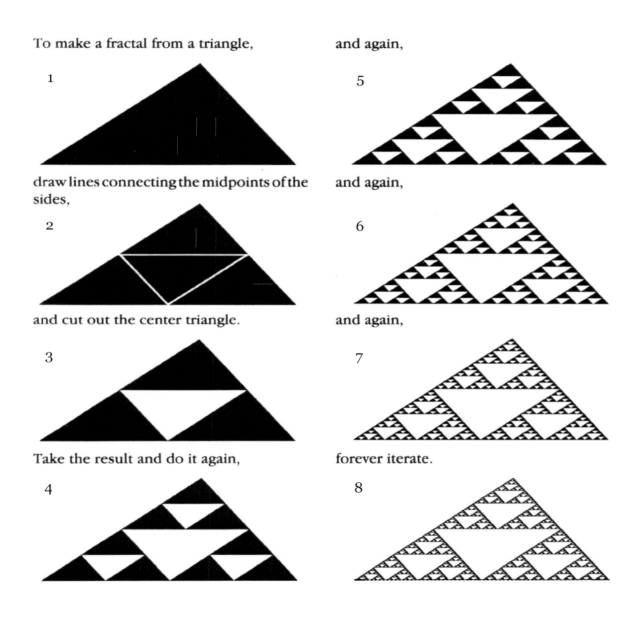

To make a fractal from a triangle,

1

draw lines connecting the midpoints of the sides,

2

and cut out the center triangle.

3

Take the result and do it again,

4

and again,

5

and again,

6

and again,

7

forever iterate.

8

Illustration A-38 -- Sierpinski gasket

number of new pieces = 3
multiplication factor = 2

D = log 3/ log 2 = 1.58

Randomness can be easily introduced into the iteration and feedback process to achieve striking images that appear natural. In *An Eye for Fractals,* Michael McGuire illustrates this by introducing randomness into the process of the development of the Sierpinski gasket. Instead of using the midpoint of the side of the triangle he randomly picks a point within a diameter of half the length of the side. After only eight iterations, he produces a very convincing mountainside with rugged rock outcrops as shown below.

The heavy lines are the result of the last iteration.

Clear the construction and make the corners black.

After eight more iterations, and enlarging:

Illustration A-39 -- Randomness introduced to the Sierpinski gasket

Except for the one utilizing randomness as part of the iterative process, the fractal curves and objects we've produced so far have exactly the same form at a descending sequence of scales. This similarity in appearance at all scales is called **self-similarity**. It is one of the general characteristics of many fractals.

61

Lengths and infinity. The next mental jump to make is to become comfortable with the idea that infinity is a part of our lives and surroundings, not only related to the unfathomably large scale of astronomy or small scale of quantum mechanics. Playing with infinity can be experienced on a personal computer with a fractal geometry program, or just a walk in the woods. To give an example of this different concept of infinity and the relationship to length in fractal geometry, Mandelbrot asks, "What is the length of the coast line of Britain?"

From the Euclidean point of view this could be considered a trivial question, but upon further consideration it reveals more complexity. Let's measure the coastline of Britain. To begin, we need a measuring stick. We'll start with one 200 miles long as shown on the right. This measuring stick shows a coastline of 1400 miles. However, this isn't very satisfactory in that a lot of variation of the coast has been smudged out by the gross size of our measuring device. Therefore, the next measurement uses a measuring stick half the size: 100 miles. Sure enough, the measured length increases to 1625 miles.

We can measure with a 50-mile stick and get 2000 miles, then a 25-mile stick and get 2,400 miles. It doesn't take long to realize that the length gets larger as we use smaller and more accurate measuring devices. We could finally get down to individual rocks, then grains of sand. We could go on into molecular and atomic levels. At some point, it becomes easiest to say that length is *attracted* to infinity. Attraction of this sort is another common concept in fractal geometry, as many lengths in fractal geometry are essentially infinite. This is the pattern of many natural forms that are generally highly fractured (Latin for *fractus*, from which the word fractal is derived).

This exercise illustrates the pluralistic nature of scale in fractal geometry. Scale is where we select to focus within an infinite choice of scales, as with the measuring devices previously mentioned, instead of a single, static measurement as in Euclidean geometry.

As a summary of this section, let's expand on our original chart about assumptions behind each geometrical system.

M = 200   L = 1400 mi.   M = 100   L = 1625

M = 50   L = 2000 mi.   M = 25   L = 2040

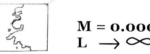

M = 0.0001 miles
L $\longrightarrow \infty$

M = length of measuring stick in miles
L = length of coastline as measured by measuring stick in miles

Illustration A-40 -- Different lengths of the coast of England

from Fractal Geometry in Architecture and Design by Carl Bovill, Birkhauser Press, 1996.

ABOUT	Basic assumptions behind Euclidean geometry	Basic assumptions behind Fractal geometry
4. **randomness**	Randomness has no place in geometry.	Randomness can be part of the form generating process.
5. **dimension**	There are three whole-numbered dimensions.	There are an infinite number of dimensions that can fill the gaps between one, two and three dimensions.
6. **infinity**	Infinity is not dealt with in geometry.	Infinity is an everyday quality and part of geometry.
7. **length**	Length is fixed and measurable.	Length is often infinite.
8. **scale**	Scale is the relative size of objects to ourselves, other objects, or systems of measurement.	Scale is where we choose to focus our attention in an infinity of choices of scales.

Scale, decisions and design. In fractal geometry, scale is pluralistic. <u>Since scale is where we choose to focus in an infinite choice of scales, we must select the scale at which to work.</u> Whether taken consciously or not, this selection of the scale of concerns is the first design decision made on any project. Most design today does not take the infinite possibilities of the scales of concern into account.

One example is a typical architectural design situation with a very constrained program and site. One could say that the scales to be considered are totally determined by the program and the physical boundaries of the site. So what choice does the designer have in regard to scale? The answer is a great deal more than most architects usually believe. If designers would broaden their focus to consider the larger climatic setting and the microclimatic possibilities of the site, they could design a passive solar building utilizing onsite energies. The rarity of recognizing this one aspect of building practice nowadays is not due to technical difficulty, but failure to identify the large-scale effects of climate on the site.

A second example is the natural and cultural history of the site. Regardless of how restricted or covered, every location has a rich natural and cultural history. Time has a scale that can be expressed in the new design that will occupy the site. Perhaps the designer can only do this by metaphor if they are otherwise constrained. Nonetheless, this opportunity should not be lost because of a failure to recognize the temporal scales of a site.

A third example is the internal scale of individuals that will use the site and buildings. As living beings we all carry around scalar relationships that have the ability to create fractal forms. An illustration of this is the pattern of walking paths shown in Illustration A-41. If not constrained by predetermined routes, humans as well as other animals will quite naturally create paths that are far more fractal than Euclidean.

Illustration A-41 -- Pedestrian paths on fallow lands in Camden, New Jersey

Form generation II: Transformational replacement.

The preceding examples used the iterative feedback process to create some of the classic fractal curves. The results are self-similar forms repeated at a potentially infinite series of scales. When randomness is introduced, we can easily create very natural looking forms of surprising complexity. To create more complexity, it is also possible to modify an object at each iteration with regard to shear, rotation or reflection. This is a specific form of transformational replacement called *linear transformation*. The result is *affine similarity*. In affine similarity, the patterns are transferred versions of the proceeding images, but not actually the same, as in self-similarity.

Koch curve with self-similarity.

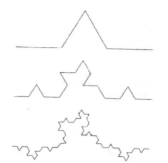

Koch curve consisting of affine similarity produced by reflecting the ⎯Λ⎯ on a random basis achieved by coin toss.

Illustration A-42 -- Affine similarity with a Koch curve achieved by linear transformation

A most intriguing thing happens when we produce form by a system of iteration and feedback via linear transformation. The original image is soon dissolved by the iterative process and becomes a form strictly determined by its original arrangement. The final image that results is called the *attractor* of the process. In many cases, universal forms start to grow out of this process.

For example, three "R" blocks placed in the order shown on the right will be attracted to our old friend, the Sierpinski gasket. An example of the surprising richness that can be produced is the fern image by Michael Barnsley, shown below.[28] It illustrates why fractal geometry is called the geometry of nature.

arrangement

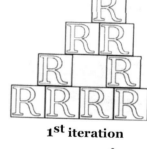

1st iteration

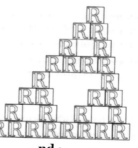

2nd iteration

eventual attraction

Illustration A-43 -- Linear Transformation

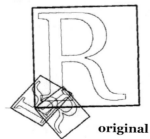

original

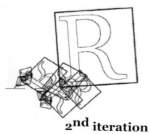

2nd iteration

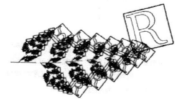

4th iteration

sufficient iteration to reach the final shape

Illustration A-44 -- Production of fern fractal form by linear transformations

[28] Michael F. Barnsley, *Fractals Everywhere*. Morgan Kaufmann Publishers, 1993.

Form generation III: Nonlinear transformation

Fractal geometry gets even more interesting once we encounter nonlinear relationships. Nonlinear refers to equations that do not plot as a straight line, but as a curve. Usually they have exponential relationships such as $y = x^n$ where n is not 1. Most relationships in the universe are nonlinear. When dealing with exponential relationships, one encounters a problem since we also have to deal with $\sqrt[n]{}$ relationships. The difficulty is that roots of negative numbers can't exist because $(-1)(-1) = 1$. Therefore $\sqrt{-x}$ cannot be a negative number. To avoid this problem mathematicians use what is called an imaginary number symbolized by i. i is defined as $\sqrt{-1}$. Therefore, negative nonlinear relationships can be addressed by using the i notation with all negative exponential numbers.

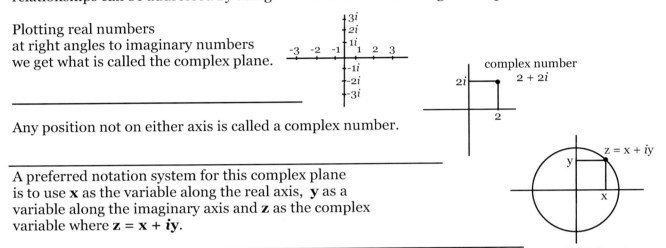

Plotting real numbers at right angles to imaginary numbers we get what is called the complex plane.

complex number $2 + 2i$

Any position not on either axis is called a complex number.

$z = x + iy$

A preferred notation system for this complex plane is to use x as the variable along the real axis, y as a variable along the imaginary axis and z as the complex variable where $z = x + iy$.

To get into nonlinear fractal geometry, let's iterate this complex number z by doing the following: $Z_{new} = Z_{old} + C$ where C = a constant value consisting of a real part and an imaginary part. Therefore, $C = a + ib$ where a = the real part and ib equals the imaginary part.

The point of all of this is that the attractor of every iteration of this equation (except for the case where $C = 0$) produces a very interesting complex fractal object.

For conditions where x is greater than 1, such as 1.1, our situation outcome is rapidly attracted to 0. Where x is less than 1 such as 0.9, our situation outcome is rapidly attracted to infinity. This is the only place where things are simple in this situation. If C = any other number, the attractions of the equation result in fantastic fractal forms called "Julia sets." These were named after Gaston Julia, who did much of this work around the turn of the 19th century. Some examples of Julia sets are below and on the next page.

 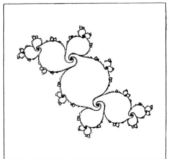 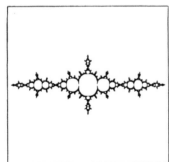

Illustration A-45 -- Julia sets

65

Znew = Z²old + C
where C =
.74543 + .11301*i*

Julia Sets of
Newton's method
applied to
E^Z = 1

<u>Illustration A-46 -- Julia Sets</u>

Source: Barnsley, Devaney,
Mandlebrot, Peitgen, Saupe,
and Voss, *The Science of
Fractal Images*. Springer-
Verlag, 1988.

Some of the Julia sets produced by iterating $Z_n = (Z_n)^2 + C$ are connected, and some aren't. If we again plot on a complex plane the equation: $Z_n = (Z_n)^2 + C,$ but this time, when the iteration produces a connected Julia set we color the point black, and when it produces a disconnected set we color it white. If we do this for enough points, within the **-2 to 2 and -2i to 2i** on the complex plane, we develop the object to the right, called a Mandelbrot set.

This fantastically complex entity is the edge or boundary between connected and disconnected Julia sets. Like the Julia set, the Mandelbrot set has infinite complexity and is characterized by deterministic chaos. Deterministic chaos means behavior is unpredictable but replicable. One cannot predetermine it, but every time it is generated, it will come out the same way. Deterministic chaos is where much of life and living things dwell, as will be explored in the next section.

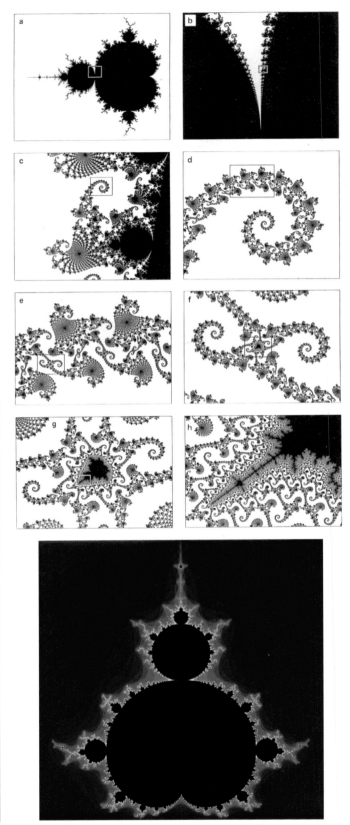

Illustration A-48 -- Mandelbrot set

Mathematics and social symbolism.
The Mandelbrot set has become an icon in the science of complexity and chaos, much to the chagrin of many scientists who feel it is impure and a misapplication to take scientific concepts out of context and into the realm of metaphor. Environmental designers, however, should know better. The establishment of basic science and its vast application in industrial society was only made possible through the application of new discoveries as social symbols. We need to only look at Renaissance architecture, planning and landscape design in some depth to understand the power and necessity of this kind of process in the dynamic of social change. The reason the Mandelbrot set became an instant icon is that, in Ian Stewart's phrase, "It is a clue towards an integrated worldview and organizing principle."[29] In this context, fractal geometry could be as important to design for a sustainable era as the rediscovery of perspective drawing was for design for the emerging scientific/industrial era in the 17th century.

---

[29] Ian Stewart, *From Here to Infinity*. Oxford University Press, 1996.

<u>Illustration A-47 -- Mandelbrot set</u>

68

A window into chaos. At the more complex levels of the iterative process, feedback and sensitivity to initial conditions become so complex that behavior becomes unpredictable and infinitely complex. Yet the process contains a perceptible order that can be exactly reproduced under the same conditions. This area of deterministic chaos is strongly connected to the more complex fractals, especially with regard to the complexity of living processes.

There are many examples of deterministic chaos: the turbulent flow of a stream, the rhythmic beating of a healthy heart, or the growth of populations in ecological systems. Let's take the growth of population, since this is a subject that will come up again when we look at historical fractal patterns of human population growth.

There are many equations used in ecology that attempt to model population growth. One of the simplest is **Xnew = (1 + R)(Xold) where R = rate of growth.** However, unless population values are unusually small in relation to the carrying capacity of the environment, population growth is typically dependent upon population density. This environmental feedback makes the equation nonlinear. In other words, **X** is effected by **X** itself, producing a X^n relationship.

Assuming there is a maximum population (**M**) that can be sustained under constant environmental conditions (still a vast simplification from most situations), our equation becomes:
R = r(M-x) Letting **M = 1**, we can scale relative to it.

Therefore, **Xnew + [1+ r(1-Xold)] Xold = (1 + r)(Xold -r X^z old)**

This equation **Xnew = (1 + R)(Xold) -r X^z old** is what we will iterate to determine the attractors at different values of **r** in relation to **M = 1**.

Similar to the previous nonlinear equations with the Julia and Mandelbrot sets, we want to run enough iterations to determine the attractor of this equation. Up to **r = 2** is predictable. Population **X** is attracted to **M** and settles into this attractor after about 50 iterations. However, where **R is greater than 2**, very interesting things begin to happen, as seen on the charts below.

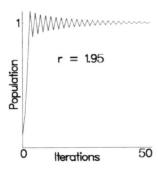

up to r = 1.95 population is attracted to 1 value.

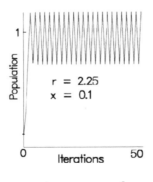

at r = 2.2 population cycles between 2 different values.

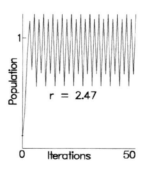

at r = 2.47 population cycles between 4 different values.

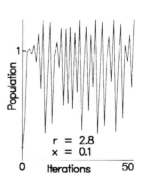

at r = 2.8, the pattern becomes chaotic.

Illustration A-49 -- Population curve at various values of r

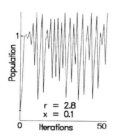

r = 2.8
x = 0.1

At 2.8, the system reaches the chaotic realm. Another way of saying this is the cycles between different values become infinite.

Now we're in the chaotic realm, with the following characteristics:

1.   It is not possible to predict the population at any number of iterations. The only way to see what it is, is to perform the equations. The system is chaotic but determinate. The results can be reproduced if the same numbers are used each time and the initial conditions are the same.

2.   Results are incredibly sensitive to initial conditions. The chart on the right starts at an r that is only one millionth different from the chart on the left, yet it is totally different. This is called **sensitivity to initial conditions.**

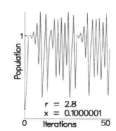

r = 2.8
x = 0.1000001

Plotting all of these cycles and attractors versus **r** gives us a nice map of the different realms of behavior of this population equation.

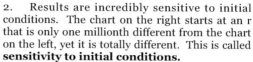

This map illustrates:

1. The connection between fractal geometry and deterministic chaos.

2. The amazing complexity that can be generated by the iterative process with very simple equations. This is the form generating process of fractal geometry.

3.   Within the chaotic realm of behavior are areas of non-chaotic behavior wherein a series of self-similar fractal patterns of bifurcation occur and start the chaotic behaviors again. These behaviors occur in an infinite progression of scales. Within this prelude to chaos, the relationships between the proportions of these bifurcations are universal constants. Universal, in that when approaching the onset of chaos, these proportional relationships are always the same regardless of the particular processes being plotted. Thus constants as universal as **π (pi)** grow from processes leading to chaotic behavior and reveal previously hidden order within the disorder of chaos. The traditional duality between order and chaos becomes a questionable abstraction.

area of attraction to M

area of cycling to 2 values

area of cycling to 4 values

areas of cycling to 8 values

non-choatic realm

choatic realm

Doubling of values is called bifurcation and is a prelude to the entry into the chaotic realm.

Areas of nonchaotic behavior with self-similar patterns of bifurcations at a smaller scale.

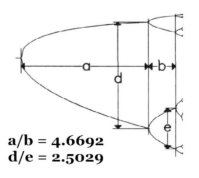

a/b = 4.6692
d/e = 2.5029

<u>Illustration A-50 -- Chaotic vs. non-chaotic realms in a population equation</u>

70

To conclude this primer, we complete the chart of basic assumptions by comparing the social implications of Euclidean and fractal geometries.

Summary A.2
    b. Cultural Implications

ABOUT	Basic assumptions behind Euclidean geometry (2000 years old)	Basic assumptions behind Fractal geometry (20 years old)
1. **description**	The main concern is the description of human-made objects. Natural objects are assumed to be difficult to describe or indescribable by geometry.	There is holistic reality, infinitely complex but geometrically describable, which we call nature.
2. **form**	Simple rules give simple forms. Complex forms require complex rules, therefore simplicity is a virtue.	Infinitely complex forms are easy to generate by simple means. Complexity is an integral part of reality and is accessible to us. Simplicity can be a virtue but can also be simplistic. Complexity is our biological heritage.
3. **form generation**	Formulae are the generator of form.	Iteration and feedback are the generator of form.
4. **randomness**	Randomness has no place in geometry.	Randomness can be part of the form generating process
5. **dimension**	There are three whole-numbered dimensions.	There are an infinite number of dimensions that can fill the gaps between one, two and three dimensions.
6. **infinity**	Infinity is not dealt with in geometry.	Infinity is an everyday thing and part of geometry.
7. **length**	Length is fixed and measurable.	Length is often infinite.
8. **scale**	Scale is the relative size of objects to ourselves, other objects, or systems of measurement.	Scale is where we choose to focus our attention in an infinity of choices of scale.
ABOUT	Social implications of Euclidean geometry (2000 years old)	Social implications of fractal geometry (20 years old)
9. **order**	Order is predictable and desirable. Disorder is unpredictable and undesirable.	Order can be very complex. Order and perceived disorder are not discrete things but often aspects of the same thing.
10. **reality**	Reality is dualistic with order and disorder in opposition to each other.	Reality is complex, diverse and holistic. Duality between order and disorder is sometimes a useful tool, often an illusion and sometimes delusion.

<u>Illustration A-51 -- Summary chart of basic assumptions and social implications behind Euclidean and fractal geometry</u> [30]

---

[30] An extension of this chart regarding the aesthetics of place is on page 124.

A. 2. Fractal Geometry
c. Process implications

Unlike scientists, designers deal with general societal trends, nuances, feelings and collective aesthetic and symbolic expressions. This can lead to traps of pure fashion on one hand, but can also force designers to develop an intuitive sense of the societal movements in which they work.

In this context, there has been a general reaction to the formalization of fractal geometry and chaos. Disbelievers, who didn't understand or disliked science, found an excuse to state that everything is unpredictable and science is overrated. True believers, convinced that science is essentially defined as prediction, denigrated fractal geometry as a passing fad of little interest. Others set to work using the insights and principles within their work. While all this will take years to settle out, there is no doubt that the social myths upon which much of the scientific/industrial cultural era was built now have an unmendably deep crack. The belief was that we (some of us at least) could be in total control, that we could predict everything given enough knowledge, or a big enough computer, or with the accumulation of enough power. This was never a reality, but it was one of the cultural myths that grew up around science and was a factor behind some of the worst excesses of the industrial era. From the perspective of our emerging sustainable era, the demise of this abstraction is an anecdote to the arrogance of which industrialized humans have been capable. This arrogance grew out of the basic assumption (taken for granted and accepted without reservation) that we can eventually predict and control everything--weather, culture, politics--rather than having to dancing creatively with chaos.

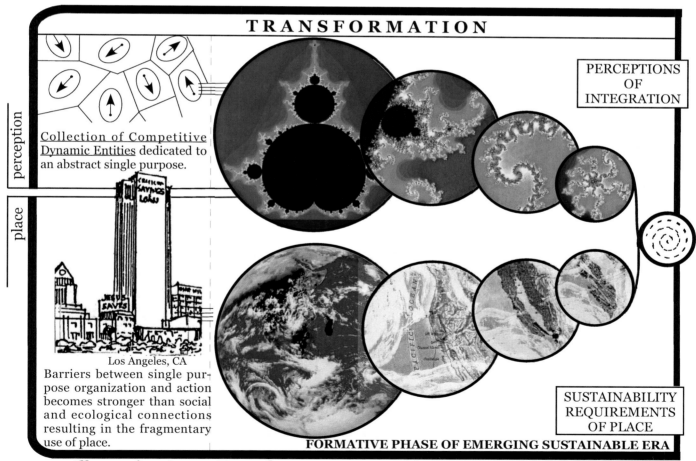

TRANSFORMATION

perception

place

Collection of Competitive Dynamic Entities dedicated to an abstract single purpose.

Los Angeles, CA
Barriers between single purpose organization and action becomes stronger than social and ecological connections resulting in the fragmentary use of place.

PERCEPTIONS OF INTEGRATION

SUSTAINABILITY REQUIREMENTS OF PLACE

FORMATIVE PHASE OF EMERGING SUSTAINABLE ERA

Illustration A-52 -- Fractal geometry as an aide to perceptions of cultural transformations

A .2 Fractal Geometry
d. Aesthetics and geometry

Introduction. Of all the arts, music seems to be the most universal in terms of provoking an aesthetic response, yet it is the least literal fit for Plato's theory of art as imitation (mentioned on page 23). Theories about music span from before Pythagoras in 400 B.C. to R.F. Voss, J. Clark and others in the present. Today, electronic devices allow physicists to make very sophisticated analyses of the structure of music. Much of this work implies that music, like many natural fluctuations in time, is fractal in nature.

Noise and music. Voss, a physicist who worked with Mandelbrot, approached the question of the structure of music through the analysis of scaling noises.[31] Scaling noise is noise that sounds the same at different speeds once the volume is adjusted. The familiar hiss of static on a radio or "snow" on a television screen are common examples. Voss studied scaling noise by doing harmonic analysis involving spectral density and auto-correlation.

Spectral density is a measure of the average behavior of random signals varying in time. In technical terms, spectral density **(sv)** of a quantity **V** fluctuating with **(t)** time = v^2 in a unit band width centered on frequency **(f)**. The average is usually taken over 30 periods. Auto-correlation measures how the fluctuations in the signal are related to previous fluctuations. The definition of these terms for our discussion is less important than what they tell us about scaling noises.

The hiss of the static on our radio produced by the random motions of electrons through an electrical resistance is called "white noise." It is a totally random sequence that can be replicated by putting musical notes on a wheel and selecting notes in a random sequence by spinning an attached marker. White noise of this type is characterized by the spectral density of **$1/f^0$**. We would get a straight line if we plot log *spectral density* versus log *frequency*, as shown in Illustration A-53.

Another scaling noise is "brown noise," named appropriately after Brownian motion. This is the random motion first noticed in the movements of small particles of dust on the surface of a liquid. Each movement is random but dependent upon its previous position. Brown noise is more correlated than white noise. Brown noise can be replicated by a similar wheel and spinner except that the numbers on it would be +1, 2, 3 etc. and - 1, 2, 3, designating the up or down movement of the next note. The spectral density of brown noise is **$1/f^2$**. If we plot log spectral density vs. log frequency, we get a steep line.

Voss and Clark measured the spectral density of music and found that, generally, it is halfway between white and brown noise, having a spectral density of **1/f.** They called this "pink noise." This is true regardless of the type of music. Voss and Clark tried classical, jazz and rock music and they all plotted the same, as shown in Illustration 53.

---

[31] Martin Gardner, "White and Brown Music, Fractal and 1/f Fluctuations," *Scientific American.* (April 1978): 16-32.

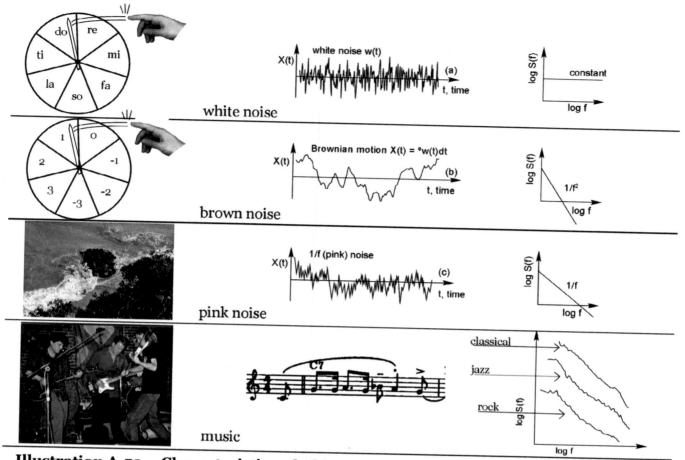

Illustration A-53 -- Characteristics of white noise, brown noise, pink noise and music

Many other fluctuations in time have been found to be **1/f** phenomena in regard to spectral density. These are things like:

- the annual flood levels of the Nile (recorded over centuries)
- variations in sun spots
- the wobble of the earth's axis
- undersea currents
- traffic flow on a freeway
- the healthy beating of a heart
- the clustering of galaxies at different scales in the universe

This led Voss to remark that "music could be thought of as imitation of the **1/f** quality of the flickering experience we perceive as a product of our environment," and "music is imitating the characteristic way our world changes in time" (score one for Plato).

Voss and Clark developed an elaborate device like the spinner used to create white and brown noise that would produce **1/f**, or "pink noise," as they labeled this intermediate phenomena. They could then mechanically produce pink or **1/f** noise and test it on listeners. Although most people agreed that pink noise was more pleasant than white or brown noise, none of it was at the level of music composed by musician. It seems that great music requires a level of involvement wherein sounds becomes an expression of emotion (score one for Tolstoy). So, perhaps both philosophers are ultimately correct but at a level of complexity they could never have imagined in their time.

Music as fractals. Kenneth J. Hsü relates music to fractal geometry through similar equations that define some of the characteristics of each.[32] As described on page 58, the equation that determined the dimensions **(D)** of fractal curves was:

$$D = \frac{\log N}{\log n}$$ Where **N** = number of pieces and **n** = magnification in the iterations and feedback form development process.

Hsü uses a similar equation for music:

$$D = \frac{\log F}{\log i}$$ Where **F** = % incidence frequency and **i** = note interval

Starting with Bach's music and proceeding through Mozart, Hsü found this equation works for much of classical music by plotting **log F** versus **log i** as shown on the right.

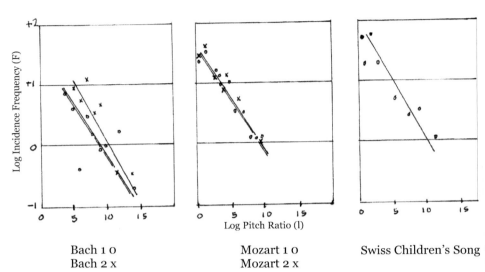

Bach 1 o
Bach 2 x

Mozart 1 o
Mozart 2 x

Swiss Children's Song

Illustration A-54 -- Fractal geometry of frequency of note intervals in music

Further studies by Hsü addressed the self-similarity of music at different speeds, which is characteristic of fractals. This applies to the fractal geometry of bird songs as well. An interesting component of the bird song studies involved varying the time scale via electronic recordings because birds have a faster metabolism than humans (and very fast songs). A bird song of ten seconds scaled up 32 times to five minutes sounds similar the first movement of a Bach concerto. These studies illustrate that time can also have fractal characteristics and that perhaps more than one species on Earth is capable of making music.

The old adage, "Architecture is frozen music," would be better stated in the context of fractal geometry as "Architecture is music at a myriad of time scales." Certainly architecture is not frozen in time. From the start of construction, the decay of buildings is a slow but inevitable process. The time of day and season bring different aspects of lighting and temperature characteristics to structures. Buildings viewed as objects frozen in space and time is an industrial era abstraction that is not only false, but so simplistic as to disconnect buildings from a great deal of aesthetic response.

Stravinsky said, "In music, only the now counts." We could say that in architecture many nows count-- short-term nows, long-term nows--all being counted at once. Architecture as an environmental art is therefore more complex, and often less pure, due to the multiplicity of users and players. However, if orchestrated well, architecture can have the aesthetic impact of music. (See Aesthetics of place, page 123.)

---

32 Kenneth Hsü, "Fractal Geometry of Music--Bird Songs to Bach" in *Applications of Fractals and Chaos,* edited by A. J. Crilly, R. A. Earnshaw, and H. Jones. Springer-Verlag, 1993: 25.

A.2. Fractal Geometry
e. Fractal architecture

Introduction. In section **A.1.d.** on aesthetics and sustainability we discussed returning to an architecture that is life-dominate. Fractal geometry shows how complex that order is—far more complex than beautifully expressing function or metaphor, or even reflecting the human condition, as in classic Greek architecture. We will have to do all of these (and more) to reunite the human condition to the planetary condition. In this regard, three concerns that are not traditional in industrial architecture are *complexity, metabolism* and an aesthetic based on *connection and fluidity*.

Complexity. Architecture for the sustainable era must celebrate rather than ignore chaotic systems and complexity. As such, it is the antithesis of the present industrial architecture. Both the pure Euclidean geometry of modern architecture and the preconceived forms of post-Modern architecture are too singular in concern to allow for meaningful complexity. Sustainable architecture is based on the realization that life is miraculously complex, that chaotic systems are the realm of life and that architecture must be part of an interplay between chaos and order, form and complexity. A healthy life can't be overly abstract or fragmentary, and neither can architecture that is healthy in its service to life.

Spatial order is one of the areas that is affected by these new criteria. Several aspects of fractal geometry are very important here. The first of these is that no object is a thing unto itself, artificially removed from its setting in splendid isolation. In fractal geometry, all objects or spaces are part of both larger and smaller compositions, tied together by self-similar or affine similar patterns. The key to working with this ideal is scale. As mentioned in the fractal primer, scale is no longer the relative size of objects or the relationships within a system of measurement, but where one chooses to focus attention among an infinite choice of scales. Absorbing this critical difference in the concept of scale is the most important step that can be made to shift from Euclidean-dominated design to fractal design. If this different perception is operational in the designer's vocabulary, we can no longer produce the disconnected, unrelated buildings so common in industrial architecture, which often resulted in buildings removed from their climatic, social, cultural and ecological settings. **The curse of over-abstraction can be cured.** Through expanding our view of design to encompass both large and small contexts, as well as designing for these scales to dance together, we will once again create great architecture.

Metabolism Me • tab • o • lis • m: 1. the complex of physical or chemical process involved in the maintenance of life (*Webster's Dictionary* 1991).

Unless you are an animist, architecture is not a living thing in the strictest sense. Yet, if it is to serve life, architecture must have some form of metabolism. In other words, it should directly respond to the physical and chemical processes involved in the maintenance of life. Industrial architecture quickly evolved to be considered merely a vessel for holding the mechanical equipment that supported the processes involved in the maintenance of life. This historical shift from an environmentally achieved metabolism to a mechanical one has had serious effects. The first is that life is too complex to be well served by complete reliance on mechanical systems, and the second is that the cost involved in the use of nuclear and fossil fuels to power this equipment is too great. With two-thirds of the energy use in the U.S. related to buildings, it has become painfully apparent how great these costs are with regard to resource use, to say nothing of the planetary effects of global warming, resource depletion and species extinction.

76

Industrial architecture was perceived as a commodity produced from resources. The impact on the larger environment of providing materials and energy was of less concern than the initial cost of obtaining them. Current economic systems are distorted by subsidies that obscure the social and environmental costs of production. In this setting, the metabolism, the process of operating buildings, is not considered. This old attitude no longer serves us, and attempts to shore up the old system are increasingly becoming a political issue. The metabolism of each building will have to become a far more important design consideration than it has been in the past.

Passive solar architecture successfully embodies the idea of making heating, cooling, venting and lighting an integral part of building design—making the metabolism of the building part of the design process. To take this several steps further, we need to consider water usage, waste disposal, sources and effects of obtaining building materials, and the health of users, region and planet as part of the building's metabolism. It is through this process that passive solar architecture evolves into sustainable architecture.

The fractal approach to scale plays an important part in this aspect of building design. Like other living beings, the metabolism of buildings is affected by things like the ratio of skin area to internal thermal loads. Buildings can be skin-dominated, like shrews and birds, or load-dominated like elephants and whales. Each of these conditions has important economic, social and environmental implications. To be a successful sustainable building, these scalar aspects should be part of the design process at the earliest phase of programming and decision-making.

A new aesthetic. In sustainable design, singular scale is replaced by a progression of multiple scales, allowing a continuity that is not obtainable in industrial architecture. In this way, we can develop a new aesthetic based on continuity and fluidity, rather than on reductionism and compartmentalization. In this context, all the basic aesthetic compositional elements mentioned in pages 23 to 32 will have to be reexamined and re-expressed.

Summary. Sustainability includes the ability to continue indefinitely without precluding other options or diminishing aesthetic, social or natural resources, which implies continuity by definition. Creating a new architecture is part of an evolution that optimizes metabolism at a continuity of scales while serving the complexity of life in a beautiful way. Hence, we are evolving mental tools to reconnect to life. This can produce buildings as well-tuned to their settings as native plants, and provide an architectural ecology that maintains and supports (rather than destroys) the natural ecology of site, locale, region and planet. Each day it becomes more obvious that we can afford to do no less.

Many architects acknowledge this need but think such an infusion of life in environmental design is unreachable. Fractal geometry shows us that complexity, integration and continuity are accessible to us. Discovering that it *is* possible is extremely important. Successful examples, such as the one described on the following pages, illustrate this possibility.

A.2 Fractal Geometry
f. example – a small cottage

Introduction. To illustrate fractal architecture as clearly as possible, we have chosen a small cottage of relatively simple functions. This straw bale passive solar cottage with 420 square feet of floor area is located near San Luis Obispo, California. Its small size allows an easier description of the self-similar relationships between setting, site, building and details as they relate to complexity, metabolism and aesthetics.

The form of the site evolved from the iterative processes of:

1. The flow of the earth: Movement of tectonic plates and the dynamics of mantle convection created a uplift of old sea bottom into Cuesta Ridge just north of San Luis Obispo, California. This is one of the first of a series of coastal ranges running parallel to the Pacific Ocean.

2. The flow of air: Present weather patterns are such that storms flow from the southwest off of the Pacific, fifteen miles away. Cuesta Ridge is high enough to cool this flow of air to induce added rainfall, but low enough that the high rainfall occurs on the leeward side at the site, a steep north slope of this ridge.

3. The flow of water: The top of the ridge is the edge of the Salinas River watershed. North of the ridge, water flows 250 miles to Monterey Bay. This flow has incised a series of deep streams above and through the site. Runoff can be chaotic in significant storms due to the steepness of the topography.

4. The flow of fire: Like much of California, fires are frequent and a natural part of the ecology. A big fire in 1994 temporarily cleared away enough vegetation that the spatial form of the land was visually apparent.

From a fractal perspective, the spatial form of the site is an attractor resulting from the iterative chaotic flows of earth, air, water and fire--the classic four elements.

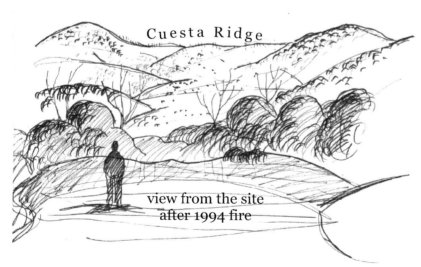

Illustration A-55 -- Location and setting

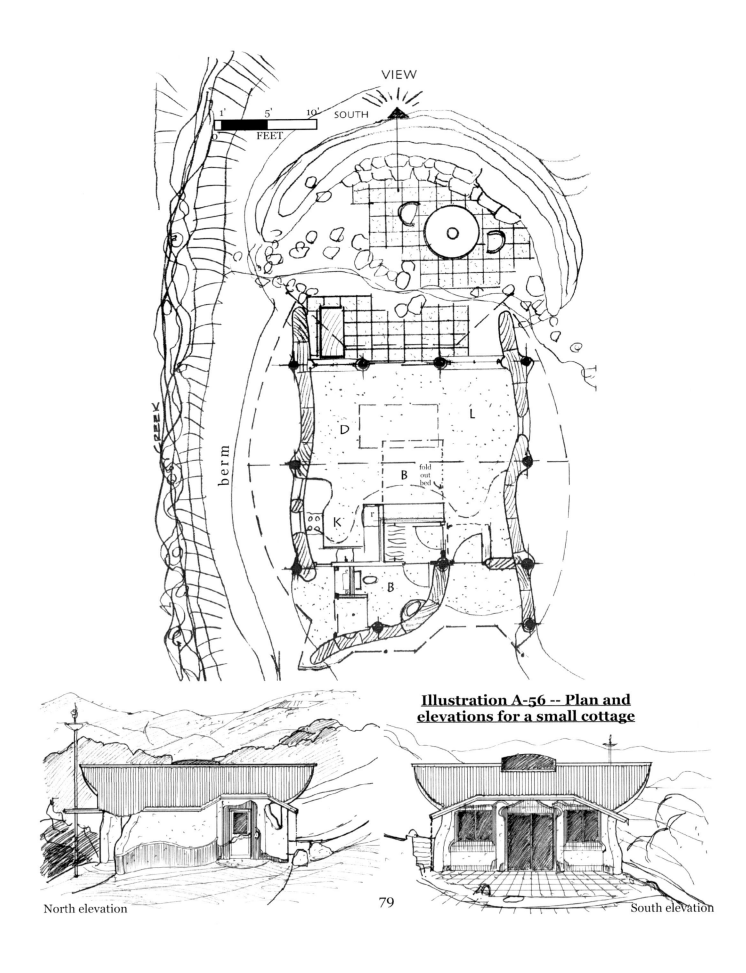

VIEW

SOUTH

1' 5' 10'
0' FEET

berm

CREEK

D

L

B
fold
out
bed

K
r

B

**Illustration A-56 -- Plan and
elevations for a small cottage**

North elevation

79

South elevation

A SMALL COTTAGE DESCRIPTION

This is a cottage for one to two people. It is small (420 square feet), but very efficient. It consists of one main room that serves as living, dining and a bedroom with a Murphy Bed that folds into the north wall. A niche on the northeast side serves as a kitchen.

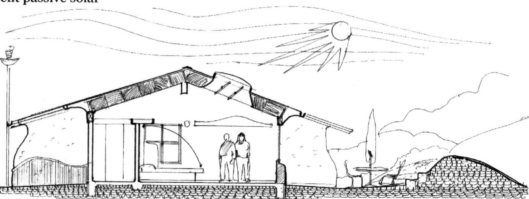

There is a separate bathroom that is entered through a dressing room and closet combination. A patio on the south edged by a four-foot berm protects the building from sudden surges of rocks and mud in case an unusually large storm energizes the adjacent creek.

The structure consists of recycled telephone poles for vertical support and two foot deep truss-joist rafters to support the roof. The walls are bales of rice straw laid on edge and curved to weave around the poles. In addition, there are wheat straw bales between the rafters for ceiling insulation. This amount of insulation helps the building act as an efficient passive solar structure. Direct solar gain is achieved by the south windows and doors and a south-facing skylight. The sky-light is insulated when necessary by a Zomeworks moveable insulated louver. Distributed thermal mass is provided by the floor slab and the stucco on the interior of the straw bale walls where the solar gain is stored. The building is independent of the power grid by using electricity from photovoltaic solar panels.

llustration A-57 -- A Small Cottage

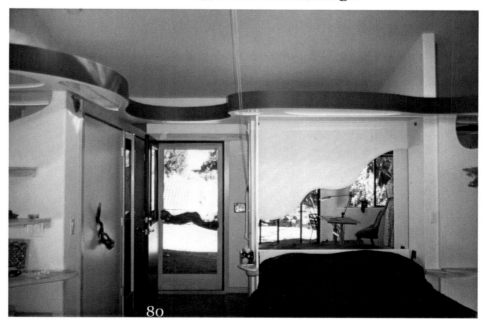

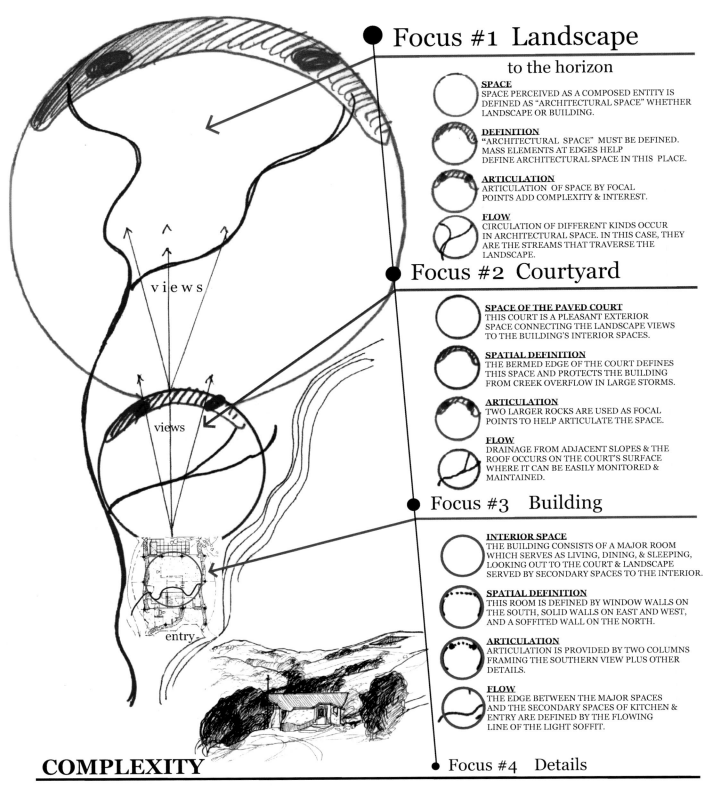

Focus #1 Landscape

to the horizon

SPACE
SPACE PERCEIVED AS A COMPOSED ENTITY IS DEFINED AS "ARCHITECTURAL SPACE" WHETHER LANDSCAPE OR BUILDING.

DEFINITION
"ARCHITECTURAL SPACE" MUST BE DEFINED. MASS ELEMENTS AT EDGES HELP DEFINE ARCHITECTURAL SPACE IN THIS PLACE.

ARTICULATION
ARTICULATION OF SPACE BY FOCAL POINTS ADD COMPLEXITY & INTEREST.

FLOW
CIRCULATION OF DIFFERENT KINDS OCCUR IN ARCHITECTURAL SPACE. IN THIS CASE, THEY ARE THE STREAMS THAT TRAVERSE THE LANDSCAPE.

Focus #2 Courtyard

SPACE OF THE PAVED COURT
THIS COURT IS A PLEASANT EXTERIOR SPACE CONNECTING THE LANDSCAPE VIEWS TO THE BUILDING'S INTERIOR SPACES.

SPATIAL DEFINITION
THE BERMED EDGE OF THE COURT DEFINES THIS SPACE AND PROTECTS THE BUILDING FROM CREEK OVERFLOW IN LARGE STORMS.

ARTICULATION
TWO LARGER ROCKS ARE USED AS FOCAL POINTS TO HELP ARTICULATE THE SPACE.

FLOW
DRAINAGE FROM ADJACENT SLOPES & THE ROOF OCCURS ON THE COURT'S SURFACE WHERE IT CAN BE EASILY MONITORED & MAINTAINED.

Focus #3   Building

INTERIOR SPACE
THE BUILDING CONSISTS OF A MAJOR ROOM WHICH SERVES AS LIVING, DINING, & SLEEPING, LOOKING OUT TO THE COURT & LANDSCAPE SERVED BY SECONDARY SPACES TO THE INTERIOR.

SPATIAL DEFINITION
THIS ROOM IS DEFINED BY WINDOW WALLS ON THE SOUTH, SOLID WALLS ON EAST AND WEST, AND A SOFFITED WALL ON THE NORTH.

ARTICULATION
ARTICULATION IS PROVIDED BY TWO COLUMNS FRAMING THE SOUTHERN VIEW PLUS OTHER DETAILS.

FLOW
THE EDGE BETWEEN THE MAJOR SPACES AND THE SECONDARY SPACES OF KITCHEN & ENTRY ARE DEFINED BY THE FLOWING LINE OF THE LIGHT SOFFIT.

COMPLEXITY

Focus #4   Details

(SEE ADJACENT PAGES)

A SELF-SIMILAR SPATIAL ORDER REPEATING THROUGH A RANGE OF SCALES CONNECTING LANDSCAPE TO BUILDING SITE, BUILDING SITE TO ARCHITECTURE, AND ARCHITECTURE TO DETAILS AND ARTIFACTS.

Illustration A-58 -- Three aspects of fractal architecture

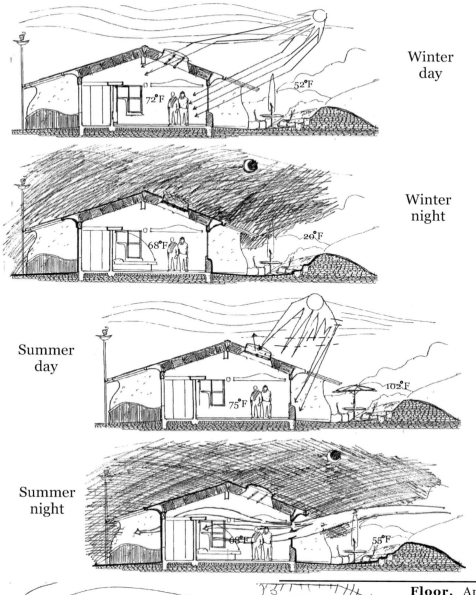

Winter day

Winter night

Summer day

Summer night

Winter heating is provided by direct solar gain through south-facing windows and skylights into distributed thermal mass. This mass consists of the exposed floor slab and the stucco on the interior surface of the straw bale walls.

Summer cooling is achieved through shading the building during the day by overhangs and movable louvers in the skylight. By night, ventilation with cool night air is used to cool the same thermal mass used to hold heat in the winter.

Embodied energy is defined as energy costs which take into account production, environmental, transportation, manufacturing, reuse and recycling costs. The embodied energy of the materials used for construction are also part of the metabolism of the building.

Floor. An existing concrete slab from a previous building destroyed by the fire was refurbished and used.

Structure. Charred telephone poles available after the fire were used for the structural frame.

Exterior envelope. Bales of rice straw were used for the exterior walls and wheat straw bales for ceiling insulation.

Wood. Most of the wood for the building came from trees killed by the fire and milled on site.

Roof. Steel roofing composed of 85% recycled content.

Artifacts and decoration. Collected glass and melted aluminum from the fire.

METABOLISM

Eighty percent of the energy used to build and operate the building is from on-site sources including passive solar heating, night-vent cooling and electricity from photovoltaic solar panels, as well as materials from close proximity to the site.

 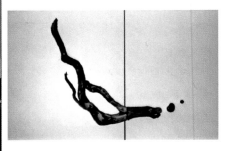

AESTHETICS

Connection and continuity are expressed in self-similar elements providing a theme of fluidity.

A.2. Fractal Geometry
g. Conclusions

Changes in the design process via fractal geometry. The major change fractal geometry brings to environmental design practice is an altered concept of scale that embraces the idea of complexity and diversity. The result, which always occurs with major changes, is a different aesthetic.

A summary of changes in the design process includes:

1. **Scale is where you consciously decide to focus within an infinite number of potential focus points (foci).**

    Singular scale in a Euclidean sense is replaced by a continuity of internesting scales. The selection of appropriate foci and their relation to region, site, people, function, materials, etc., is an integral part of the design process and is not given by fiat. These are choices that must be made by the designer.

2. **Metabolic efficiency is measured by the use of the smallest range of foci.**

    Using the nearest possible foci for energy, materials, water and waste processing allows miniaturization of present metabolic processes and the greatest efficiency of the whole. Accordingly, the designer must work as much as possible with on-site resources, and minimize the use of off-site resources.

3. **Aesthetic effectiveness is measured by the expression of the broadest range of foci within the design.**

    The broader the reach of the design, the more obtainable the aesthetic goals of continuity and connectivity become. This is in contrast to the aesthetic expression of reductionism and compartmentalization characteristic of industrial architecture. A fractal contextualism must be an integral part of the aesthetic composition.

4. **Complexity can replace the importance of function.**

    Once functions are distributed to the appropriate foci, spatial complexity can be central to the design. If a design is completed with an intelligent and complex series of scales, all the necessary functions can be provided for and will ensure the evolution of the design over time.

5. **Affine or self-similarity is the glue between parts and wholes, variety and unity.**

    The integration of each complimentary aspect—nature and urbanity, work and retreat, community and privacy—should occur at each foci in a pattern of self-similarity, or affine similarity, where perceived contradictions can be resolved.

6. **Maximum social and cultural diversity is possible and desirable within a cohesive unity.**

    In fractal geometry, infinite diversity and unified order is an everyday occurrence, not an idealistic dream. The design must enhance, not diminish, diversity.

Introduction to the Contexts section. We are at a "make-it or break-it" point in human evolution--a transition that has occurred only three times before in worldwide human history. This transition involves a shift in the basic relationships of environment, resource base and responsive human organization. The first of these transitions was the slow evolution of hunting and gathering cultures, the second was the more rapid evolution of cultures based on agriculture and husbandry, and the third was our relatively rapid evolution into a scientific/industrial culture. From the broadest perspective, each of these eras contains a formative phase, an optimistic florescence, a mature or classic period and finally a stressful period where cultural problems create hardship, pessimism and social dysfunction. These periods of stress also produce the impetus for the necessary effort to invent and design the next period. Several indicators point to the fact that we are at such a pregnant point in history today. (See page 89.)

Environmental design, like any other human endeavor, reflects this general evolutionary pattern. The late part of the 19th century saw the tentative formation of new ideas about art and architecture culminating in an amazing florescence at the turn of the century. This happened as new materials and techniques became available from industry that coalesced with new aesthetic concerns. The late 1920s and early 1930s saw a maturation of planning, design theory and technique based on industrialization, labeled "Modernism," which swept the world in the 1950s and 1960s. Finally, there was the "Post-Modernism" of the late 1970s and 1980s that reflected the stressful phase of the industrial era and a loss of faith in industrialization. The characteristics of Post-Modernism are the same as similar stages that occurred in preceding eras. These characteristics include both a nostalgic regard for the past and a highly refined abstraction and expression that numbed the perception of problems in the present, while yearning for the golden age of times past.

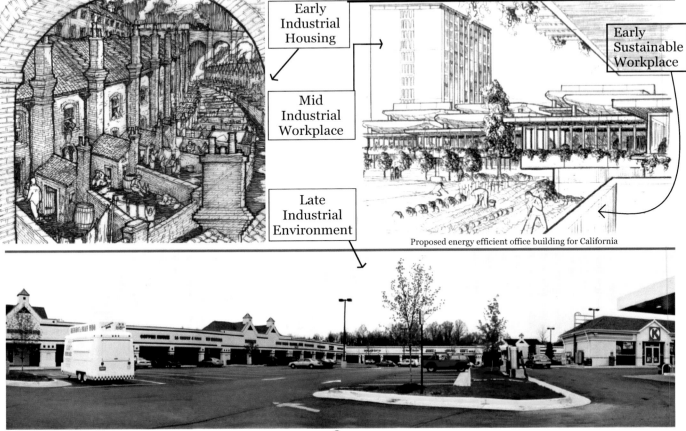

Early Industrial Housing

Mid Industrial Workplace

Late Industrial Environment

Early Sustainable Workplace

Proposed energy efficient office building for California

So, here we are hurtling into the next era with a resulting architecture that has yet to be defined. If we look deeply enough we will see this definition is already dictated by existing circumstances. **The next period of human evolution must be an era of sustainability.** Outgrowths of our industrial society, such as information technology, can be woven into a sustainability program. Our numbers, our effects on the worldwide environment, and the dire results that threaten all speak to what we must do.

What will the architecture of this era be like? How will it have to perform based on the existing indicators? How can we creatively respond to the stresses and the opportunities of transition? These questions are the starting point for this section, exploring the contexts of time and place. This much we can be sure of--architecture for this era will be as different as industrial-era architecture was from agricultural-era architecture. Nothing should be taken for granted. Every aspect of environmental design should be rethought, especially the fundamental assumptions upon which industrial era design has been based.

Early Sustainable Housing

Looking north from the common house

Looking south from the common house

Common House

Tierra Neuva Cohousing, Central Coast, California

MINIATURIZATION OF TOPOGRAPHY BY PLATE TECTONICS CREATES A RICH MIX OF CHAPARRAL, SAVANNAH AND XERIC PLANT COMMUNITIES AT THE PINNACLES NATIONAL MONUMENT IN CENTRAL CALIFORNIA.

B.1 Time
a. Fractal time and history

Introduction: Fractal time and history

Knowledge of the history of environmental design can provide us with an understanding of what the focus of design has been and inspiration for where we are headed. Knowledge of history, however, is a double-edged sword. What can provide inspiration can also become an excuse for slavish copying, which often occurred in the 19th and early 20th centuries. It can also be used as the trappings for an authoritarian program of conquest and war, as in the case of fascist Italy and Germany in the late 1930s and early 1940s, or as a façade that ignored basic human needs, such as occurred with much of the Post-Modern architecture of the 1980s.

Because we are able to view time in a fractal manner, similar to how we view space, history can be examined as a set of self-similar patterns at different time scales.

HISTORY OF HUMAN POPULATION LEVELS

Examining worldwide population growth illustrates how history can be viewed in a fractal manner as well as provide clues about the future. Plotting worldwide population versus time on a linear scale produces the first chart shown in Illustration B-1. This chart doesn't tell us much except that our numbers have reached or are fast approaching unsustainable levels. The conclusion is simple and inescapable.

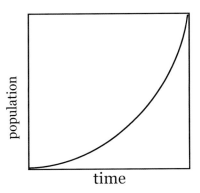

Linear Plot of History of Human Population

If we plot worldwide population levels versus time on a logarithmic scale rather than a linear one, a series of patterns emerge at different time scales that are self-similar.[33] This can be seen on the second chart in Illustration B-1 (as introduced on pages 13 and 14). What can we deduce from these patterns? We are essentially plotting the degree of successful reproduction relative to the potential reproductive capability of our species. It reveals the development of three distinct culture eras. It also shows the history of how environmental feedback from our use of resources affects cultural eras.[34]

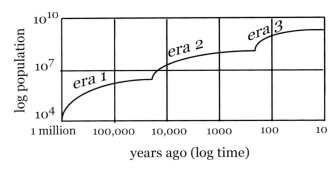

Fractal View of the History of Human Population

Illustration B-1 -- History of worldwide human population growth plotted linearly and plotted logarithmically

---

33 Edward S. Deevey, "Human Population" *Scientific American* (September 1960), 194-204.

34 R. W. Kates, "Sustaining Life on Earth" *Scientific American* (October 1994), 114-122.

A highly simplified picture of the basic relationships between population, resources and environment is shown in Illustration B-2. Energy and resources are drawn from the environment and utilized by the human population. Design decisions including the invention of technical devices, establishment of social organization and development of communication enhance the ability to extract energy and resources and determine how the population as a whole will utilize them.

These relationships can be visualized as a dynamic system that has its own lifespan. At the beginning of a successful design development (one that provides more energy and resources than were previously available), times are fat. Relatively large amounts of energy and resources are available to a relatively small population. There is usually a period of experimentation where trial and error are needed to develop the designs that provide these advantages, but once successfully synthesized, the system's success can be dynamic and result in relatively rapid population growth. We can call such a period in history a formative period evolving to fluorescence.

As design techniques are formalized and the population expands, systems tend to become comfortable and relatively static. Such a period can be referred to as a classic period. At this point, however, the population is now large enough that pressure on the environment has increased, causing changes that can affect the available resources. If a society is to maintain itself, some design efforts must moderate this pressure on the environment. Techniques for obtaining energy and resources are fixed into relatively static patterns, and social and cultural patterns are adapted to moderate population growth and more obviously destructive behaviors.

<u>**Illustration B-2 -- Lifespan phases of a cultural system**</u>

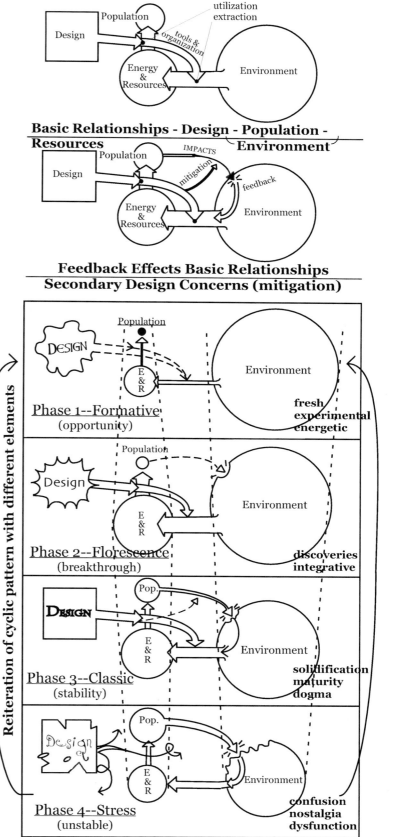

Basic Relationships - Design - Population - Resources - Environment

Feedback Effects Basic Relationships
Secondary Design Concerns (mitigation)

Phase 1--Formative
(opportunity)

fresh
experimental
energetic

Phase 2--Florescence
(breakthrough)

discoveries
integrative

Phase 3--Classic
(stability)

solidification
maturity
dogma

Phase 4--Stress
(unstable)

confusion
nostalgia
dysfunction

Reiteration of cyclic pattern with different elements

As the population continues to grow, pressures on the environment and inevitable chaotic changes in climate can cause destructive feedback from the environment, which is the source of available energy and materials. As this continues, the entire system enters a period of stress. Societal and cultural dysfunction becomes more common. Anthropologists have traditionally called this a decadent phase. If enough stress occurs, the whole system will collapse or be replaced by an entirely new system.[35]

At the very largest scale, plotted in Illustration B-3, this pattern has happened three times in human history. These are indicated by the three bumps on the chart. The steep inclines of the bumps are the formative and fluorescent phases of a particular cultural era, the top of the upward curve is the classical phase, and the relatively flat areas are periods of stress. Here the population is still growing, but at a significantly lower rate than our capacity to reproduce.

By now it may be clear what these periods of human history are. The first is where energy and resources were obtained through **hunting and gathering,** the second is the era of **agricultural and husbandry,** and third is the era of **science and industrialization.** This chart was first published thirty-four years ago.[36] By that time, the handwriting was already on the wall with regard to where the Industrial Revolution was headed.

From this chart we see that the environmental crisis is not new, **but a recurring part of a self-similar pattern when viewed on a global scale.** The first human environmental crisis occurred about 12,000 years ago as hunting pressure and climatic changes killed off most of the large herds of animals in what is now Europe, North America and Australia (by people we tend to consider as ecologically sensitive).[37] The second crisis occurred 5,000 to 2,000 years ago as the great agrarian breadbaskets of the world were slowly destroyed by salinization of the soil through long periods of irrigation, deforestation and erosion from over-grazing. We are now in the midst of a third great environmental crisis as a result of industrialization with its accompanying worldwide pollution, warfare and ecologically disruptive policies.[38] The problems of each crisis seem unsolvable when viewed from within each cultural era and context. Certainly, our problems seem unsolvable from our industrial-era perspective. But, as in the last two periods of transition, they will be solvable if viewed from the context of the new era that follows: The era of **information and sustainability. Perceptions precede solutions, and pioneers should be valued.**

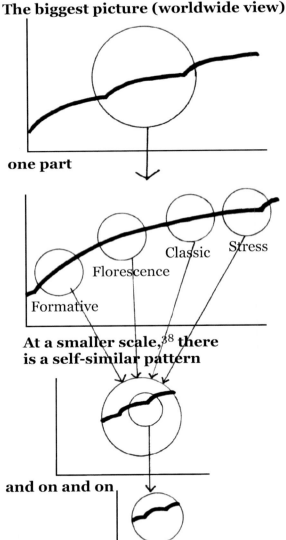

The biggest picture (worldwide view)

one part

Classic Stress

Florescence

Formative

At a smaller scale,[38] there is a self-similar pattern

and on and on

Illustration B-3 -- Self-similarity in patterns of cultural eras

35 Jared Diamond, *Collapse--How Societies Choose to Fail or Succeed,* Viking Press, 2005. An extensive analysis of numerous societies that have destroyed their immediate environment and therefore themselves, contrasted with other societies that have been sustainable for thousands of years.

36 The chart was published in Edward S. Deevey, "Human Population," *Scientific American* (September 1960), 194-204.

37 R. Monster Sky, "Ancient People Sparked Die-offs Down Under," *Science News* (Jan. 1, 1999), 155.

38 Steven Mitren, *After the Ice.* Harvard University Press, 2004. This book describes in great detail some of the smaller scale patterns in the transition from hunting and gathering to agriculture and husbandry.

An interesting nuance is the relationship of the preceding eras as the new era comes into existence.[39] Hunting and gathering did not go away when the agricultural revolution occurred. It was redefined in the social and cultural context of agriculture and husbandry. Hunting, for example, usually became a sport--only permitted to nobility. Likewise, agriculture and husbandry did not disappear with the advent of the Industrial Revolution; they were redefined in the cultural context of industrialization. Similarly, in the era of sustainability all three of these methods of obtaining energy and resources must be redefined. We must reinvent hunting and gathering, agriculture and husbandry, science and industry. A shift in geometrical thinking will be a part of this process.

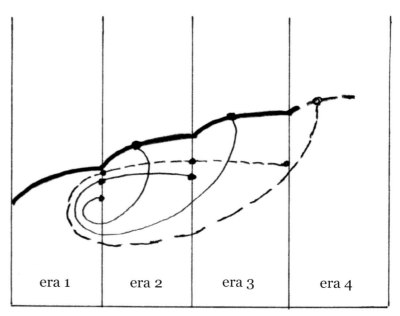

Illustration B-4 -- Redefinition of preceding by each succeeding era

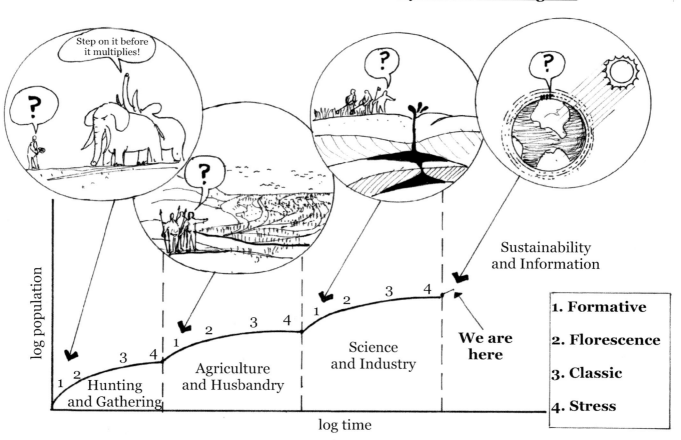

Illustration B-5 -- Indicators of epochal change

39 Bill McKibben, "A Special Moment in History," *Atlantic Monthly* (May 1998), 55-78.

B. 1. Time
b. The history of environmental design

Introduction. The pattern discussed in the last section is at the largest scale from which we can view human population growth. Because of this, unique variations that occur within each time period become blurred. In this lost detail are amazing variations of some localized instances. One example is the sophisticated agroforestry practice of native Californians that is often confused with a hunting/gathering culture. For original Californians, native oak trees were the staple of their diet, just as grain had become for Europeans, who had long ago forgotten their own oak agroforestry history.[40] In addition, variations are evident between different areas of emphasis within the same era, such as the relationships between agricultural people and herding people, both of which are stage two cultures. Lastly, these cultural eras occurred at different times and places.

As with any fractal view, the more closely magnified iterations have more variations when viewed at smaller scales. There is evidence that early forms of both agriculture and industrialization were so stressful to the constituent population that the lifespan and reproductive rates temporarily dropped rather than rose. All these variations are interesting at the scale at which they occur, but aren't visible at the global scale, shown in Illustrations B-1 through B-5.

With the current speed of communications and transportation, the large-scale consideration provides a more apt description of today's world. This, plus the transition to a new cultural era that is occurring, means that this big pattern could be the basis for a more holistic look at the history of environmental design. Such a perspective would approach our rich history with a more systematic examination of the ecological and cultural basis for all settlement patterns, architecture and artifacts. This should allow for a more equitable emphasis on each cultural era and location without preconceived cultural, ethnic or regional bias.

In contrast, the present approach to environmental design history generally takes a quick look at a few sacred places from our hunting and gathering past, such as Pleistocene cave paintings in Europe, and then jumps right into the classic large scale hydraulic civilizations. Monuments are emphasized over settlement patterns and vernacular architecture. Not only does this isolate a small part of the picture, it ignores cultures where vernacular and monumental architecture are similar. Two good examples of this are classical Era 2 Islamic and Japanese cultures. Agriculturally-based civilizations are usually emphasized at the expense of husbandry-based ones in spite of the fact that a husbandry-based culture created the largest empire in the second cultural era—the Mongolian Empire of the 13th and 14th centuries. Climate change and ecological factors are seldom discussed, in spite of our increasing awareness of their significance. Some of the more sustainably oriented cultures in harsh locations such as in the Himalayas are rarely mentioned. A final problem is the emphasis on European history at the expense of much of the rest of the world. The rich cultures that occurred in Africa, pre-Columbian Americas and Oceana are only cursorily examined, if at all.

Updating design history to a sustainable-era perspective would transcend these problems by providing a more holistic and diverse picture. The shift in mental framework necessary to understand the periods of transition of each cultural era would help clarify where we are today as we evolve from an industrial to a sustainable era.

---

[40] Glen Martin, "Keepers of the Oaks" *Discover* (August, 1996), Vol. 17, #8: 45-50.

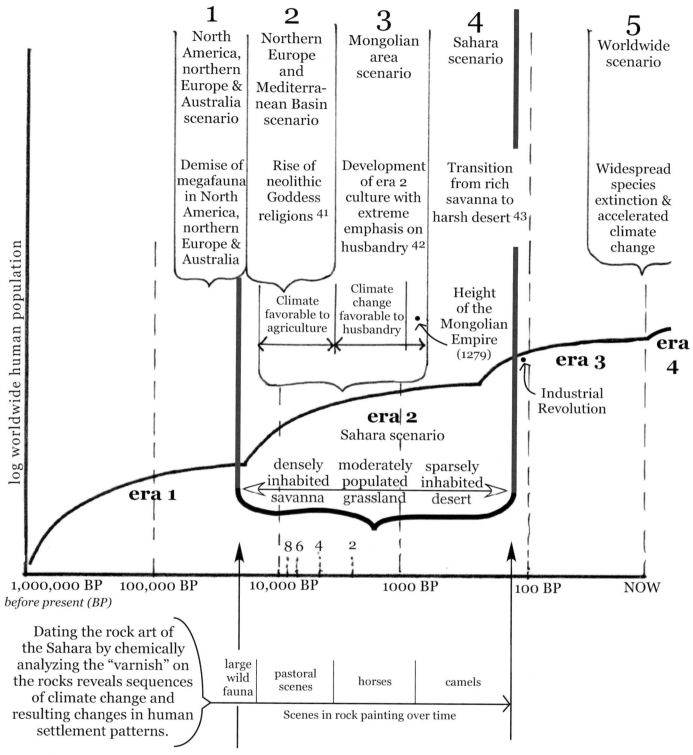

Illustration B-6 -- Contextual placement of five specific historical scenarios

[41] Leonard Schlain, *The Alphabet versus the Goddess: The Conflict Between Work and Image,* Penguin Compass, 2004.

[42] Jack Weatherford, *Genghis Kahn - The Making of the Modern World,* Crown Publisher, 2004.

[43] Forte and Siliotti, *Virtual Archeology,* Abrams Publishing, 1997.

History with an emphasis on continuity and diversity. The diagram on page 96 illustrates a holistic view of environmental design history. It locates historical examples by where they fall between the poles of conceptual design and evolutionary design. There are several advantages to this:

1. It gives equal emphasis to all three previous cultural eras. The transitions between different eras are given the emphasis they deserve. For example, in transition 1, conceptual design was more earth and nature oriented and therefore relevant to our present time--transition 3. Era 2 examples were ethnically based, although some of the larger empires were to some degree multicultural. This ethnicity in Era 2 is replaced by a host of different schools in Era 3 that are determined more by philosophy.

2. It gives equal emphasis to vernacular design as to monumental or conceptual design. In many periods the two were quite separate, as can be seen in this view of the Mesopotamian city of Ur in about 3000 B.P.

3. It illustrates the relationship between various styles of architecture. Of particular interest are periods of transformation when a particular direction transcends its roots to become both conceptual and evolutionary. These are shown by an elliptical circle and star on the diagram.

4. It also illustrates the life cycles of different movements. This pattern that repeats many times is a beginning, growth and eventual decay of vitality. Eventually idealism becomes cynicism, passion becomes just 'the way things are done,' an emphasis on basics ends up ignoring basics. Many schools start with a reasoned rationale that decays into thoughtless formulas. This process can have great subtlety, however, some general patterns are clear. The beginnings usually start at the evolutionary side of the diagram and end up at the conceptual side. Concepts gradually become frozen, leaving a shadow on the evolutionary side of early vitality no longer in evidence. An example from the industrial era is the fading of the International School. As it lost currency by becoming static in concerns and caught in the successes of the past, it left a shadow of its original vitality at the evolutionary pole.

5. The end of each era is marked by very abstract conceptualizations that are increasingly disconnected from the ecological setting. Part of this process involves nostalgia for so-called better days, resulting in revivals of various sorts. Results of this over-conceptualization are the Baroque, Rococo, Mannerist and Neo-classical styles at the end of Era 2. At the end of Era 3, this process resulted in increasingly diluted revivals of revivals. The most recent of these styles that infects the outgoing industrial era, particularly in North America, is the "trophy vernacular." This may be perceived at first glance as a contradiction. Trophy implies a high level of disconnection and abstraction involving only one concern, while vernacular implies a common unquestioned way of doing. All this is far removed from the vernacular of earlier periods.

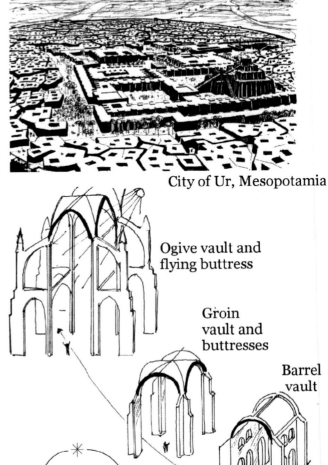

City of Ur, Mesopotamia

Ogive vault and flying buttress

Groin vault and buttresses

Barrel vault

Gothic   Romanesque

Evolution of Gothic architecture from Romanesque by the invention of the Ogive vault by Abbé Suger in 1234.

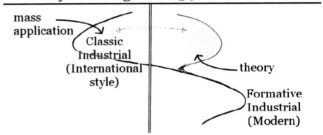

mass application

Classic Industrial (International style)

theory

Formative Industrial (Modern)

Illustration B-7 -- Details of chart on the next page

95

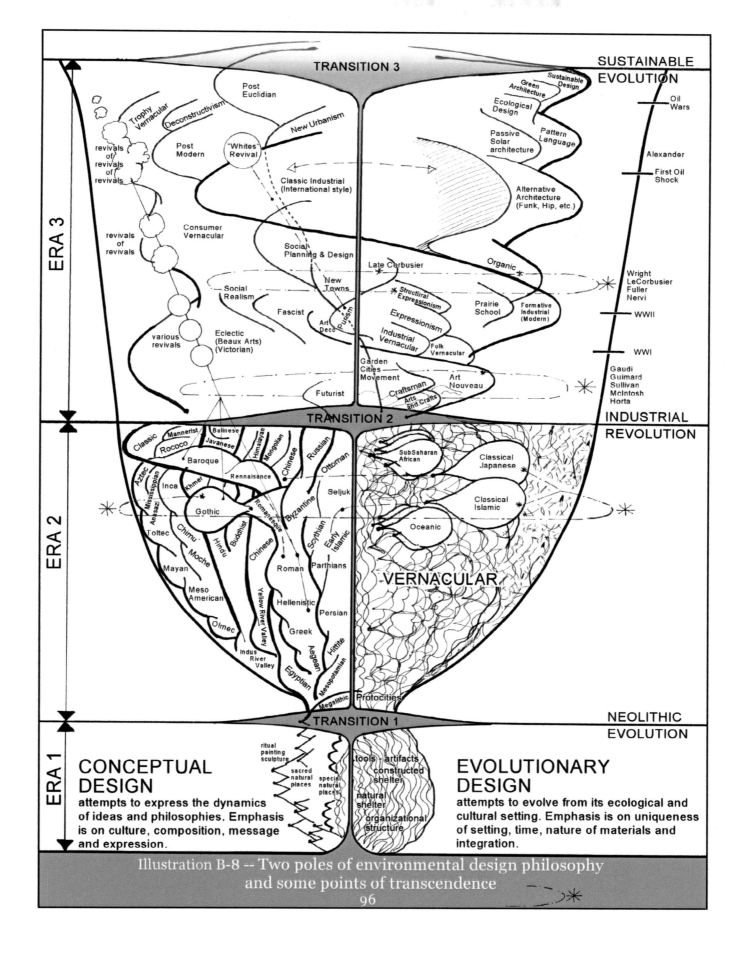

Illustration B-8 -- Two poles of environmental design philosophy
and some points of transcendence

96

B.1 Time
c. Historical transformations
d. Aesthetics and symbolism

Introduction. Social transformations are the result of many complex factors. They can be the result of changes in knowledge, economic conditions, philosophical or religious framework, and technological conditions. Environmental design is strongly affected by these transformations and is often a part of the change since aesthetics and symbolism are integral to the cultural condition of the time. Thus, these transformations influence design, which in turn influences the transformation. These relationships can be clarified by looking at a few historical examples. Shown below and to the right is a brief graphic glimpse of environmental design symbolism in three such transformations. Two are historical examples from Europe and the other is from the present.

Generally there are two major causes of such transformations. Modified perceptions about reality constitute one cause and are shown diagrammatically on the upper band of the illustration. The other cause is new design requirements of place due to social change, shown on the lower band. One cause is conceptual and the other is practical. Changes in planning and design theory can come from either one of these causes, or from both at once.

An additional consideration is how ideas are communicated. Since planning and design involves many people, success or failure can depend to a large degree on communication. A change in perception of reality inevitably involves description. Description can enhance or reinforce, but it also modifies the perception itself. When they are successfully transmitted, perception, description and communication can merge into a cultural expression. It is this cultural realm in which planning and design must operate.

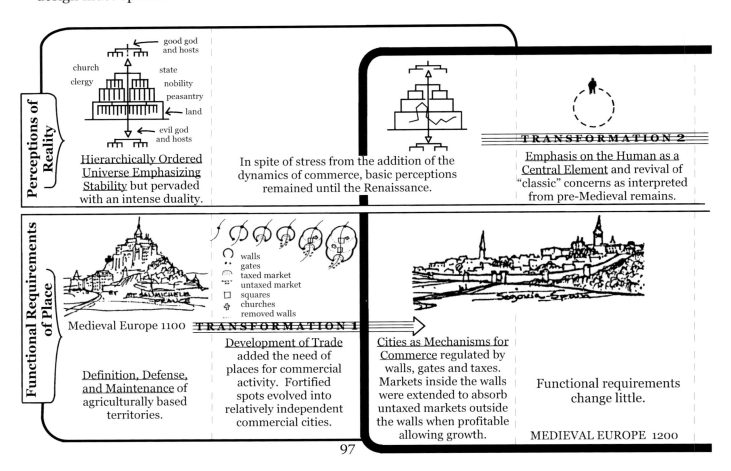

Symbols during transformations. Images can also become symbols. Symbols express emotional reality and are not literally descriptive. They can be an extraordinarily powerful means of cultural communication.

An example of the use of symbols can be found in the transformation from the late Medieval period to the Renaissance (transformation 2 on the chart below). The harsh application of Euclidean geometry to design and eventually to city planning symbolized the changes in perceptions embodied in Renaissance culture. Euclidean geometry became the symbol for the rebirth of humanism, and the basis of Renaissance planning and design. This was in contrast to the earlier, more organically evolved geometric order of the Medieval period. Medieval cathedrals, for example, were far more sophisticated and technologically advanced than the Renaissance design that followed, but their symbolic power was greatly weakened as the geometric basis of perceptions changed.

Symbols operate the same way today, conveying certain emotions at a cultural level, which we do not often consciously recognize. One of the best symbols of our late industrial period is the television advertisement. It provides scant literal information, but in its aggressive, concentrated singularity of purpose, totally fragmented from larger concerns, it is a powerful expression of a period we can no longer afford.

Illustration B-9 -- Brief illustration of three culture transformations

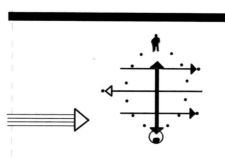

Matrix of Centered Relationships with Human, the Perceiver, as the Main Element.

Humanist perceptions were expressed by a geometrical order of axial relationships to focal points. The whole was made predictable by the newly rediscovered geometry of perspective. Bilateral symmetry was reflective of the human body. Control by the viewer over natural elements was expressed.

Loosening of medieval system allowed more experimentation. The stage is set for the later development of reductionist and mechanistic viewpoints.

EARLY RENAISSANCE 1300

TRANSFORMATION 3

Collection of Competitive Dynamic Entities dedicated to an abstract single purpose.

Los Angeles, CA

Barriers between single purpose organization and action becomes stronger than social and ecological connections resulting in the fragmentary use of place.

LATE INDUSTRIAL ERA 1945-2000

Transformation in planning and design theory today. Any period of history has positive and negative aspects. What many of us perceive as the worst faults of the late industrial era--the isolation of individuals, weakening of the social fabric, exploitative mining of the environment and robbing resources from future generations--are the end products of what was seen as positive change in previous periods. Unlike the dualistic Medieval perception of good and evil, positive and negative are not fixed in eternal, celestial isolation. They are relative to circumstances and the strange mix each era produces. The emphasis on commercial growth, individualism, human domination of nature and the rationalist scientific method of "isolate, classify, and evaluate" have, in addition to their past successes, helped to bring us to the place where our entire planet is threatened.

This situation forces us to modify the meaning of functional requirements of place. We have come to consider place as a thing to be molded to our own needs. Hence, the great emphasis on function in industrial-era architecture. But now we are beginning to see that place has needs of its own.

In the early Middle Ages, holding territory or place had obligations of defense and maintenance. This concept has been lost and needs to be revived--not in a medieval way, but in a manner appropriate to our time. Our place, our environment, obliges us to provide for sustainability at a fractal cascade of scales from individual to planetary. At the same time, our perceptions are beginning to change because of the continued evolution of science. Relativity and quantum mechanics are contributors to this change, but from the viewpoint of planning and design, these changes in perception consider only the very small and the very large and are quite remote. The science of complexity and emergence, however, deals more directly with the scale of everyday experience. It completes a link in a trinity of new perceptions, which, along with the concept of sustainability, will transform planning and design theory.

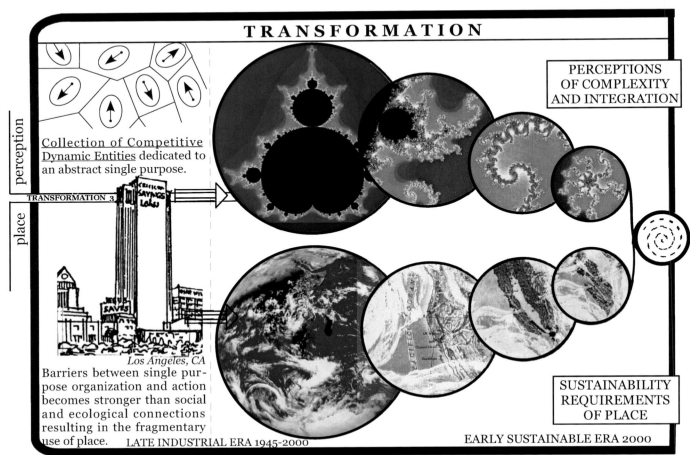

TRANSFORMATION

perception

place

Collection of Competitive Dynamic Entities dedicated to an abstract single purpose.

TRANSFORMATION 3

PERCEPTIONS OF COMPLEXITY AND INTEGRATION

SUSTAINABILITY REQUIREMENTS OF PLACE

Los Angeles, CA
Barriers between single purpose organization and action becomes stronger than social and ecological connections resulting in the fragmentary use of place.

LATE INDUSTRIAL ERA 1945-2000

EARLY SUSTAINABLE ERA 2000

B.1. Time
e. Prototypes of sustainable design

Introduction. In the preceding part of this book it was proposed that achieving a sustainable culture requires a cultural framework that implicitly recognizes and celebrates that:

1. Reality is a <u>unity</u> that has infinite variety.
2. We should have "<u>scalar integrity</u>" where parts affect the whole and vice versa.
3. <u>Harmony</u> between wholes and parts is possible **and** desirable.
4. <u>Expression</u> is joyous and is a critical part of making things work.

In many ways the cultural environment of our late scientific/industrial society does just the opposite:

1. Great emphasis has been given to the power of circumscribed analysis while neglecting the losses due to the resulting fragmentation of reality.
2. We have made a cult of individualism while paradoxically producing scalar conditions where the individual feels powerless to affect the whole.
3. Conflict and struggle are glorified while harmony is underplayed.
4. Expression is suspect, art is seen as bohemian activity cast adrift, an outcast activity that is not integral to society.

The enormity of our problem is that we find it difficult to imagine, let alone to develop, the more sustainable attitudes necessary to transcend our present dysfunctions. Therefore, precedents are extremely important--not to copy, but to illustrate the potential, the desirability and the richness possible in a more sustainable culture. The precedent analyzed here is in Bali, a small island in the Indonesian Archipelago. Bali is a powerful precedent because historical and geographical circumstances and human creativity have produced a culture that is a beautiful expression of the principles of unity, scalar integrity, harmony and aesthetic expression. Bali's historically rich culture has evolved into an agricultural/tourist economy without destroying this heritage. As a result, it is not a museum of an older sustainable society, but a living contemporary example of evolutionary sustainable design.

B.1. Time
f. Example: Bali—A prototype of sustainable design

The physical characteristics of Bali are such that a unified system of topography, hydrology, agricultural patterns and settlement patterns are very efficient and plainly apparent. This allows the island to support a dense population and rich culture and art. Each scale is integrated into the whole of the island, creating a miniaturized grain that allows an optimized human environment. This system is illustrated in the fractal scan on the following pages.

Bali is a small island, approximately 130 miles across. It is dominated by the holy volcano, Mount Agung, at 3142 meters in height. It is the largest of a series of volcanic peaks with rich soils, occasionally "renewed" by volcanic eruptions. These mountains also catch rain and the resulting runoff creates a sloping plain, serrated with arroyos, where most of the human activity takes place.

The small square shows the area to be examined at the next smaller focus.

Focus 1
The Whole Island

On pages 21 and 22, miniaturization was discussed with regard to information processing and thermal control of buildings. Urban and architectural space can also be miniaturized. Bali is a living example of this miniaturization possibility. This allows a very high population density with the buildings being no more than 2-3 stories in height while supporting a high quality of life.

This is possible because of integrated design relationships from the settlement pattern scale, shown in Focus 2, to the architecture and artifact scale, shown in Foci 3 and 4.

Illustration B-10 -- Fractal Scan view of Bali
(pages 101 - 104)

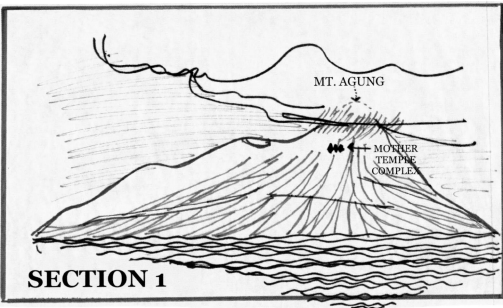

At this scale, the key to gaining efficiency is the fine grain of three urban components. These consist of pedestrian lanes, rice paddies and arroyos. Each of these components are separate enough to have their own character and work efficiently, but close enough to avoid over-reliance on transportation. Therefore, pedestrians and bicycles can dominate the circulation system. Longer range and heavier load transportation needs are met by the use of Bemos, which are small trucks similar to pick-up trucks, often with seats so they can act either as buses or cargo haulers.

Focus 2
The Town of Ubud

This system of arroyos and lanes create a very fine-grained spatial order in which agricultural and architectural patterns occur. Rice paddies border the arroyos and buildings border the lanes. The arroyos serve a variety of purposes including a complex irrigation system, linear open space, swimming and washing pools and reserves for natural vegetation. They occur so regularly that everyone has easy access to them. They are steep enough to make crossing them difficult. Hence, most roads occur in a north-south direction perpendicular to the arroyos. The few cross-roads that do occur tend to concentrate activity and become more urban in function and character.

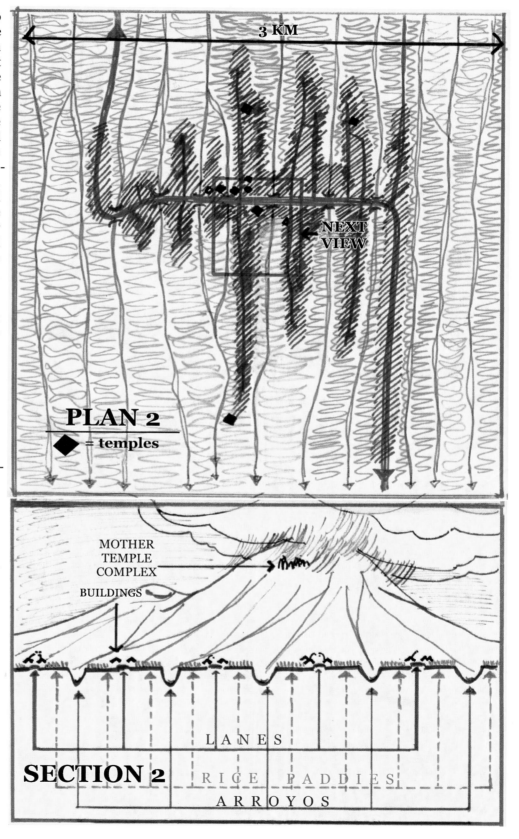

3 KM

NEXT VIEW

PLAN 2

◆ = temples

MOTHER TEMPLE COMPLEX

BUILDINGS

SECTION 2

L A N E S

R I C E   P A D D I E S

A R R O Y O S

The three urban components of lanes, paddies and arroyos serve many overlapping functions. Lanes are for circulation, but also serve as commercial, social, and ceremonial spaces. The paddies serve as open space of a garden nature, growing rice, grazing ducks and raising frogs. Overlapping uses ensure it is not a monocultural agricultural operation. The arroyos serve as drainage, but also as more natural open spaces with large trees, big rocks, bathing pools and places of solitude (which are important at such high population densities).

Focus 3

Center of Ubud

Buildings are small-- usually two stories at most. Many activities occur outdoors due to the benign climate. Living units consist of several buildings, home temples and storage facilities. Large overhangs, insulating thatch roofs and the fine spatial grain allow for maximum natural ventilation to provide comfort in hot, humid weather.

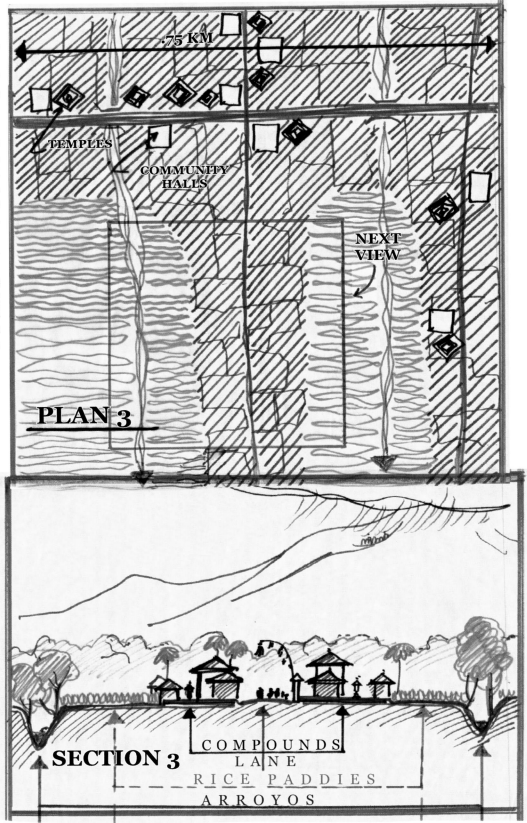

.75 KM

TEMPLES

COMMUNITY HALLS

NEXT VIEW

PLAN 3

SECTION 3

C O M P O U N D S
L A N E
R I C E   P A D D I E S
A R R O Y O S

103

Within this pattern architectural and artifactual patterns occur. Most people live in compounds that face the lanes and open to them through gates. The buildings that comprise these compounds are quite small, so it is easy to develop outdoor spaces between them. Living spaces consist of both indoor and outdoor space appropriate to the climate. These spaces allow privacy for the family and a place for the family temple. The temples are usually so small they are at an artifactual scale. The lanes are decorated from time to time with artifacts related to ceremonies.

Focus 4
Family Compounds

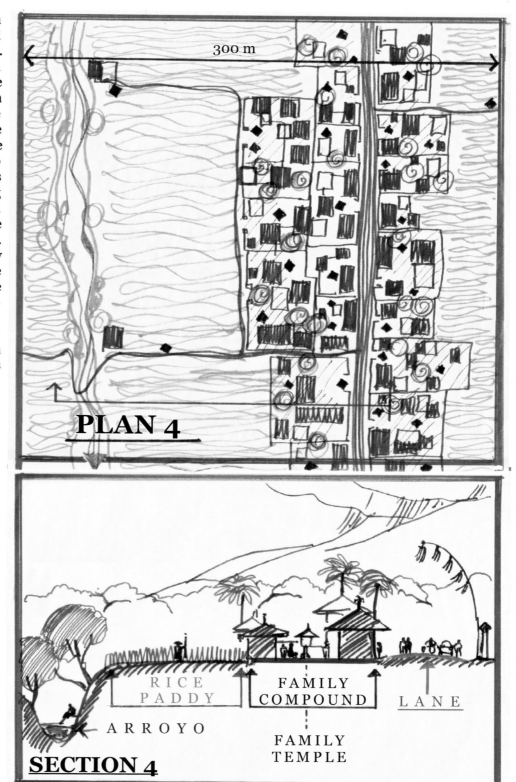

300 m

PLAN 4

SECTION 4

RICE PADDY

FAMILY COMPOUND

LANE

ARROYO

FAMILY TEMPLE

Philosophical characteristics. Philosophical characteristics are most concretely expressed in a formalized religious structure, a form of Hinduism uniquely adapted to Balinese conditions. The structure of this religion is pluralistic and multi-focal with emphasis on diversity, exuberance and unity. It is a structure that suits the rich florescence of this tropical island. From the viewpoint of sustainability, the religion fits the ecological setting and reinforces one's relation to that setting through ritual and celebration.

The temples that serve Balinese Hinduism are rich and complex compounds consisting of many buildings, spaces, towers, gates, sculptures and occasionally, lakes. In this sense, they are elaborate versions of the living compounds of ordinary people. Temples permeate the society in another example of the progression of descending scales discussed earlier. At the largest scale is the "mother" temple complex, Besakih, located at the base of Mt. Agung, the volcano which is both the symbolic and literal source of the island and the runoff water which maintains life. From this temple complex, a series of huge platforms usually drenched in rain, one can look out over the verdant plain of arroyos, rice terraces and villages to the sea and see the closed cycle of continuous regeneration that comprises the life support system of the island.

Next in scale are large temple complexes throughout the island in sacred locations, followed by multitudes of smaller temple complexes existing in each village. Further down in scale are smaller temple compounds in the countryside and smaller villages. Always existing in conjunction with these temples are roofed, open pavilions available for public activities such as temple fairs, dance performances, rehearsals or just lounging around. At the smallest end of this progression, temples exist in most living compounds. They are tiny buildings, usually only 4 to 7 feet in height, but are very carefully and artfully constructed of stone, brick and thatch.

The rituals held in these temples deal with the entire life cycle. Even death is not considered the end or a transfer to some more perfect place, but a form of recycling. To mark the freeing of the soul for rebirth and the recycling of the body, elaborate cremation ceremonies are held. These are not somber events, but maintain a festive air. If the family is able to afford it, the body is paraded through streets in an elaborate tower with music and a large crowd of friends, neighbors and tourists. At the arrival to the cremation ground, the body is placed in a large black paper maché bull and then burned. Aside from the appropriate send-off, this religious ritual has the practical function of not wasting valuable agricultural land for graveyards and employs many people to create the mobile architecture used in the ceremony.

Illustration B-11 -- Cremation Parade - Bali 1988

105

Social characteristics. The social organization necessary for designing and maintaining the elaborate infrastructure systems of Bali has created a society that emphasizes cooperation and social harmony. This cooperative ideal is reinforced by religious practices that are festive in nature and involve many people. The fine arts also illustrate this theme of cooperation. Paintings generally are jammed with figures associating with one another. Performing arts are very participatory and highly coordinated. Often performances require so many musicians, dancers and singers that performers outnumber spectators. In contrast to our society, most high architecture is public in nature. Temple compounds are continuously open, and sculptures are placed along lanes and at crossroads with a minimum of vandalism. It is helpful for us to be reminded that this is possible as part of a sustainable social context.

Psychological characteristics. It is vastly easier to perceive and creatively respond to systems larger than ourselves if we are secure and reasonably comfortable with regard to our own inner ecology. Therefore, a healthy psychological environment is as important as any other element in achieving a sustainable society. The Balinese give great emphasis to the psychological aspects of their culture. They have been very successful in developing sophisticated techniques to illuminate and process human emotions.

The diversity, complexity and depth of the human condition is openly acknowledged, explored and humorously processed in a broad spectrum of Balinese arts. A simple illustration can be found in the masks that abound in Bali. The whole range of human emotions is exquisitely executed in masks of fear, insecurity, empathy, envy, love, anger, self-satisfaction and joy. Multitudes of emotions with endless nuances are realistically caught, displayed and explored through this art form. These masks are just one illustration; similar explorations occur in sculpture, painting and the performing arts. Where some cultures are loathe to acknowledge some aspects of human nature, the Balinese make it easier for people to accept and process them through art.

Permeating all this is a keen sense of humor. Humor insures against the danger of taking portrayals literally rather than symbolically. For example, no matter how horrible the demons in dances appear (and some are truly horrible looking), there is always a humorous aspect to them or a plot that gives them a human dimension. This humor allows performance to remain a symbolic expression of the human condition rather than a literal or moralistic one—the distinction between art and propaganda is maintained.

Art in Bali is not merely a collection of objects of self-expression. Art has been developed to the level of social and psychological technology that helps a sustainable culture flourish.[44]

---

[44] Miguel Corarrubias, *The Island of Bali*. Alfred Knopf, New York, 1937.

Webster's Dictionary gives the following definitions:

technology -- any practical art utilizing scientific knowledge.
science -- knowledge possessed as a result of study and practice.

Art is the glue that ties the ecological, philosophical, social and psychological aspects Balinese society
together. Art is better glue
than worldly accumulation because
it is at the level of fine art where
duality is transcended:

where parts versus whole
       becomes parts *and* whole;
where tradition versus innovation
       becomes tradition *and* innovation;
where content versus technique
       becomes content *and* technique;
where material versus spirit
       becomes material *and* spirit;
where sacred versus secular
       becomes sacred *and* secular and
where limits versus growth
       becomes limits *and* growth.

Illustration B-12 -- Temples at Besakih - 1988

It is through becoming harmoniously creative within the limits of their environment that the Balinese
have grown to explore the infinite variety available in philosophical, social and psychological aspects
of reality.

Implications of Bali as a prototype for a sustainable society. How can Bali be a prototype
with such stark differences in climate, culture, scale and economic conditions from our own? There
are equivalent situations now present in both cultures that are prerequisites for sustainability.
Consider the following:

    a. An equivalent to the Balinese celebration of "infinite variety within unity" can be found in
fractal geometry where, via computer iteration, we can explore infinite variety within the unity
of a fractal image.

In both cases, the principle of "unity with diversity" can be experienced and understood, and as such,
it is up to the task of achieving sustainability.

    b. An equivalent to standing at Besakih looking out at the closed cycle of the renewable
Balinese environment is seeing the earth via satellite.

In each case, the scalar integrity of parts-to-whole becomes recognizable, and the necessity of
sustainability obvious.

    c. Our culture typically has no humor or joy, especially in public places. In spite of our
sophisticated technology, we have not yet developed the arts as "arts of connection" that
promote harmony with ourselves, our fellows and ultimately our environment.

B. 1. Time
g. Conclusion

During the classical phase of the industrial era (late 1950s in the United States), environmental design, aside from product design and civil engineering, was not considered to be as important as it had been in earlier periods. In a society dominated by mass production of goods and an environment dominated by suburban development, it was not very clear how useful regional planning, urban design, architecture and landscape architecture could really be. Buildings could be designed by an engineer, developer, or contractor and the energy needs provided by mechanical mass-produced equipment with materials produced by the chemical industries. Cities seemed to be obsolete and landscape could be purchased as a commodity.

A look at the history of human population, resource use and environmental effects as fractal patterns reveals how critically important environmental design really is for our unique time in history. This is illustrated by the relationship of design to the basic population, resource and environment systems as shown in Illustration B-13. Environmental design must expand its concerns to be equally involved with all three aspects in such a system. Instead of solely emphasizing production, as has been the pattern in the industrial era, our emerging sustainable era must emphasize all three-- production, use and impact. The social mechanisms to ensure this on a larger scale are now in the formative stages. Many interesting ideas have been proposed.45

Each of our preceding cultural eras had two aspects--hunting *and* gathering, agriculture *and* husbandry, and science *and* industry. One had an informational context, the other, an application context. For example, science produces the knowledge that, practically applied, allows industry to conduct business. Our emerging era is information *and* sustainability. Information technology gives us the capacity to weave together the production, use and environmental impact aspects of design decisions.

Illustration B-13 -- The place of design in the periodic reinvention of culture

45 Peter Barnes, *Who Owns the Sky? Our Common Assets and the Future of Capitalism.* Island Press, 2001.

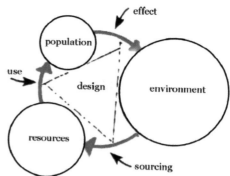

Relationship of Environment, Resources and Population

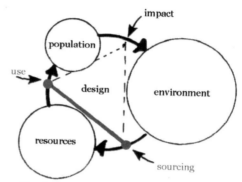

Design Emphasis of Industrial Culture

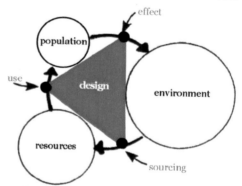

Design Emphasis of Sustainable Culture

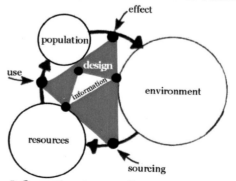

Information Aspect of Sustainable Culture

THE GREAT PLAINS GRASSLAND BIOME ONCE DOMINATED THE CENTER OF THE NORTH AMERICAN CONTINENT. IT NOW REMAINS IN SMALL PROTECTED AREAS, FALLOW LAND, ROADSIDES AND UNDER THE SURFACE AWAITING REGENERATION.

THE CONTEXT OF PLACE

B. 2 Place
a. Introduction: Our dynamic fractal planet

For many of us, it is hard to realize how new the idea of a dynamic earth is. Before the proof of plate tectonics, the discovery of periods of mass extinctions and the documentation of global climate change, the earth appeared to be a very stable, relatively static place. Even geologists believed that changes in the earth's surface were effected only through an exceedingly long process occurring over millions of years, a theory called "Uniformitarianism." It was easy to think one could take, extract and even pillage without too great an impact on the planet. The assumption was that resources would always be there—the earth was too vast and change occurred too slowly to be much affected through human activity. It was felt we could afford disconnected behavior that flew in the face of natural processes. Until the 1980s, for example, nuclear power plants were built close to active earthquake faults without much concern.

Now we know this assumption is far from the truth. A series of stunning discoveries in astronomy, geology and ecology have revealed how dynamic, complex and integrated our planet and its environs are. We now know enough of the structure of our solar system to see these dynamic processes occurring on other planets and moons as well. We can see how these processes are related to large-scale cycles of life as well as to cataclysmic extinctions. An example is the comet collision that caused the demise of the dinosaurs and the beginning of new opportunities for mammals 60 million years ago; and that was only the most recent of five great periods of extinction. We are also discovering how ubiquitous life is. It exists under the Antarctic ice cap, high in the earth's atmosphere, deep in the rock far below the surface of the earth; most likely in meteorites knocked into space from Mars and perhaps on some of the moons of Jupiter.

We know that the climate of the earth is far from static, fluctuating between warm periods and ice ages. Some of these fluctuations were very long in duration, but some were surprisingly abrupt. We are finding that we affect these chaotic cycles, and that we are in a dance of chaotic, co-evolutionary change with the earth. If we are artful in this dance we can be successful. If not, we can become extinct like many other forms of life before us.

Historically, acceptance of the earth's dynamic characteristics has been resisted. Some theologians still shun the idea of biological evolution. Some corporate leaders still resist the idea of global warming. However, overwhelming evidence makes this resistance look increasingly illogical. Far more people are aware of the dynamic aspects of the earth than in the past. However, that the earth's dynamic patterns are fractal in nature is less acknowledged.

Environmental design must increasingly become a part of the intricate chaotic dance of our planet if it is to be part of the web of life and not the husk of a parasitic organism. With this realization comes awareness of the power for environmental design to be a positive part of our co-evolutionary dance with place. The following section touches on a few of the earth's dynamic processes and what they mean to environmental design.

b. The Cosmic Ecology

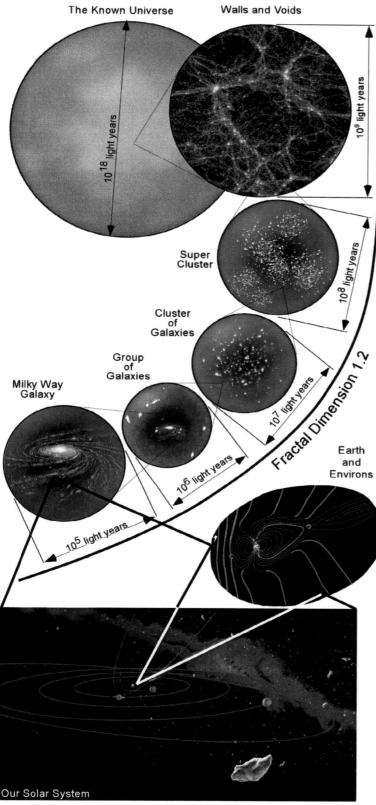

The Known Universe

Walls and Voids

10^{18} light years

10^9 light years

Super Cluster

10^8 light years

Cluster of Galaxies

10^7 light years

Group of Galaxies

Milky Way Galaxy

Fractal Dimension 1.2

Earth and Environs

10^6 light years

10^5 light years

Our Solar System

Illustration B-14 -- The Cosmic Ecology

The universe we can measure stretches out in progressively larger structures.[46] The ones shown on the left are of equivalent "clumpiness" of fractal dimension (about 1.2).[47] Only recently have we learned enough so this can be thought of as an ecological as well as cosmological system. Stars have a definite life and death, and their destruction creates the elements necessary for life. These materials are transported by various dynamic processes that allow life to evolve and prosper.

The knowledge of our solar system has expanded beyond the orderly clockwork Newtonian model to include complexity, relativity and chaos. The Kuiper Belt and the Oort Cloud, which extend about 1/5th of the way out to the next solar system, are part of this new knowledge. These entities contain millions of comets consisting mostly of ice. Ice at this extremely low temperature takes an amorphous form which, unlike ice on Earth, carries rather than rejects organic compounds.[48] If knocked into a chaotic orbit, these comets can seed the inner planets with water and organic compounds necessary for life. They can also be very destructive, as were the ones that have are believed to caused large extinction events (see pages 119-120).[49] Jupiter plays an important role for Earth as a shield that attracts enough of these comets to make these events less frequent for the middle planets.[50]

Shown here is a diagram of solar wind, the earth and our magnetosphere. The dance of these forces make our planet a complex electrical as well as material object.

[46] Stephen Landy, "Mapping the Universe." *Scientific American* (June 1999), 39-45. Graphics by Don Dixon.

[47] Richard Voss, "Fractals in Nature" in *The Science of Fractal Images* by Barnsley, Devaney, Mandelbrot, Peitgen, Saupe, and Voss. New York: Springer Verlag, 1988, pgs. 21-70.

[48] D. Blake and P. Jenniskens, "The Ice of Life." *Scientific American* (August 2001), 285, No. 2, 44-51.

[49] Tom Gehrels, "Collisions with Comets and Asteroids." *Scientific American* (March 1996), 90.

[50] Martin Rees "Exploring Our Universe and Others." *Scientific American* (December 1999), 44-49.

The Planetary Ecology

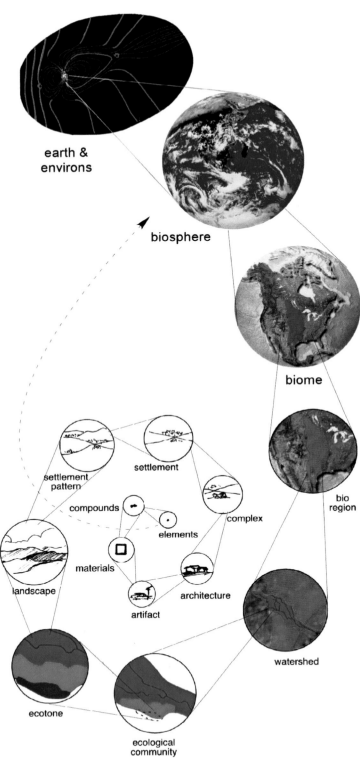

earth & environs

biosphere

biome

bio region

settlement pattern

settlement

compounds

complex

elements

materials

architecture

artifact

landscape

watershed

ecotone

ecological community

Illustration B-15 -- The Planetary Ecology

The structure of planetary ecology can be perceived as an interesting series of scales. These are the scales of environmental design and they are very important in helping to clarify where we are and how we connect to place.

Biosphere: The realm of life on Earth. From the upper atmosphere to deep into the Earth's surface,[51] life exists and thrives in an area larger than previously thought.[52]

Biomes: The major types of natural environments. Each biome consists of similar climatic, geological and ecological characteristics that are considered unique.[53] UNESCO's Biosphere Reserve Program lists fourteen terrestrial biomes and the Koppen system of world climates lists seventeen.[54]

Bioregions: Biomes further differentiated by topography, hydrology, smaller climate variation or other factors are called bioregions.

Watersheds: The area drained by a particular drainage system is called a watershed. Large watersheds contain progressively smaller watersheds. Water is such a critical element for life that watersheds are an important design consideration.

Ecological community: This is a much more specific area describing the particular flora and fauna of a biome or bioregion.

Ecotone: The overlapping areas between ecological communities are called ecotones. Ecotones are important because they are usually biologically richer than a single ecological community due to the edge effect.

Landscape: The visual surroundings as perceived by a viewer. In this context, it refers to the perceptual whole rather than vegetation.

Settlement pattern: Human settlement patterns are more diverse than the industrial standards of city, suburban and country; thus the use of this more generic term.

Settlement: A particular part of the general settlement pattern, usually politically or spatially defined.

Complex: A group of buildings, open space and infrastructure creating a recognizable unit.

Architecture: Buildings and adjacent spaces.

Artifacts: Human-made objects.

Materials: That from which a place or object is constructed.

Compounds: Building blocks of materials.

Elements: Building blocks of compounds. Compounds and elements can take solid, liquid or gaseous forms and thus can flow back into the larger entities. If done in a non-designed, careless way, this can be in the form of waste or pollution. If done in an optimized design, they can take the form of a useful resource.

[51] Josie Glausiusz "High Life." *Discover* (March 2001), Vol. 22 No. 03.

[52] J. Fredrickson, and T. Onstott, "Microbes Deep Inside the Earth." *Scientific American* (October 1996), 101-104.

[53] "Biosphere Reserves" *UNESCO publications.*

[54] Charles Bennett, *Man and Earth's Ecosystems* New York: John Wiley and Sons, 1975, 22.

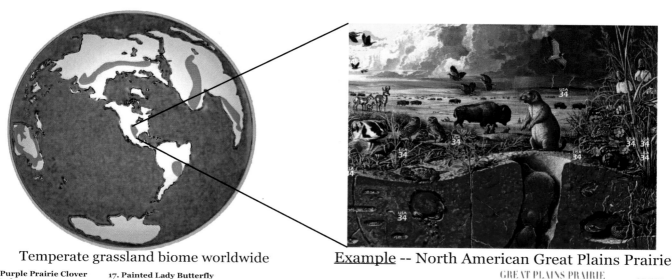

Temperate grassland biome worldwide   Example -- North American Great Plains Prairie

1. **Purple Prairie Clover**
   Dalea purpurea
2. **Canada Goose**
   Branta canadensis
3. **Pronghorn**
   Antilocapra americana
4. **Badger**
   Taxidea taxus
5. **Buffalo Grass**
   Buchloe dactyloides
6. **Harvester Ant**
   Pogonomyrmex occidentalis
7. **Burrowing Owl**
   Athene cunicularia
8. **Eastern Short-horned Lizard**
   Phrynosoma douglasii brevirostre
9. **Plains Pocket Gopher**
   Geomys bursarius
10. **Sharp-tailed Grouse**
    Tympanuchus phasianellus
11. **Bison**
    Bison bison
12. **Wild alfalfa**
    Psoralea tenuiflora
13. **Black-tailed Prairie Dog**
    Cynomys ludovicianus
14. **Swainson's Hawk**
    Buteo swainsoni
15. **Plains Spadefoot**
    Spea bombifrons
16. **Prairie Rattlesnake**
    Crotalus viridis viridis

17. **Painted Lady Butterfly**
    Vanessa cardui
18. **Prairie Coneflower**
    Ratibida columnifera
19. **Prairie Wild Rose**
    Rosa arkansana
20. **Dung Beetle**
    Canthon pilularius
21. **Little Bluestem**
    Schizachyrium scoparium
22. **Ord's Kangaroo Rat**
    Dipodomys ordii
23. **Two-striped Grasshopper**
    Melanoplys bivittatus
24. **Camel Cricket**
    Ceuthophilus pallidus
25. **Western Meadowlark**
    Sturnella neglecta

Illustration B-16 -- North American grassland biome and ecological community

Present state

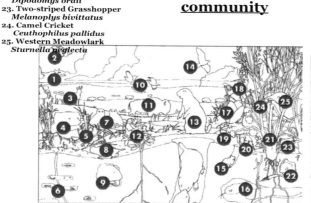

Let's put back the pieces.

It's a common misconception that the frontier in the continental U.S. disappeared in the 1890s. In fact, the North American Great Plains prairie frontier never really disappeared, and after three cycles of boom and bust, it is actually expanding. The density standard for frontier status was defined in 1890 as six persons per square mile. Loss of population after three cycles of boom and bust has caused 397 counties in this seven state region to qualify for frontier status. In the 2000 census, Kansas had more frontier counties than it did in 1890. The whole region shown in red (which is 1/6 of the land area of the continental U.S.) had 6.5 million people in 1990, barely the population of Georgia, outlined in red.

In hindsight, the quick settlement and vast ecological disruption of the Great Plains turned out to be a 150-year-long mistake--both in environmental and in economic terms. In 1987, two geographers, Drs. Frank and Deborah Popper, proposed the regeneration of the Great Plains under the metaphor of the "Buffalo Commons."[55, 56] This would be the biggest step to redefine America since the Alaskan purchase. It could restore an ailing biome of great character and beauty and could potentially help convert the demographic and economic decline of the region since now, unlike the 1890s, intact environments have great economic value. [57, 58]

55 Drs. Frank & Deborah Popper, "The Buffalo Commons as Regional Metaphor of Geographic Method." *Geological Review.*
56 Great Plains Restoration Council, *www.gprc.org/buffalocommons.html*
57 Nicholas D. Kristof, "Let the Buffalo Roam in American Midwest." *International Herald Tribune,* October 31, 2003.
58   John G. Mitchell, "Change of Heartland." *National Geographic* (May 2004), 2-53.

Cultural Ecology. Place is a cultural as well as physical entity. We carry culturally derived aspects of place with us, and they manifest themselves, quite automatically, in our social response to space. Anthropologists[59] have documented how diverse and strong this response can be, even with regard to simple things like the social spacing of two people involved in conversation.[60, 61] The Modernist approach to environmental design has largely ignored the cultural ecology of place, which, because of its narrow rationality, emphasis on technology and the scale and speed of application, has often had destructive consequences (see page 29).

Illustrated below and on the next page are five classic agriculture/husbandry-era cultures expressed in diagrammatic form to show cultural characteristics of place. The sixth diagram illustrates a "classical" scientific/industrial culture. These diagrams may appear simple, but when viewed in depth they reveal patterns basic to specific cultural ecologies.

59 Ruth Benedict, *Patterns of Culture,* New York: Houghton Mifflin, 1934.

60 Edward T. Hall, *The Hidden Dimension*, New York: Doubleday, 1966

61 Paul Oliver, *Shelter and Society,* London: Barrie & Jenkins, 1976.

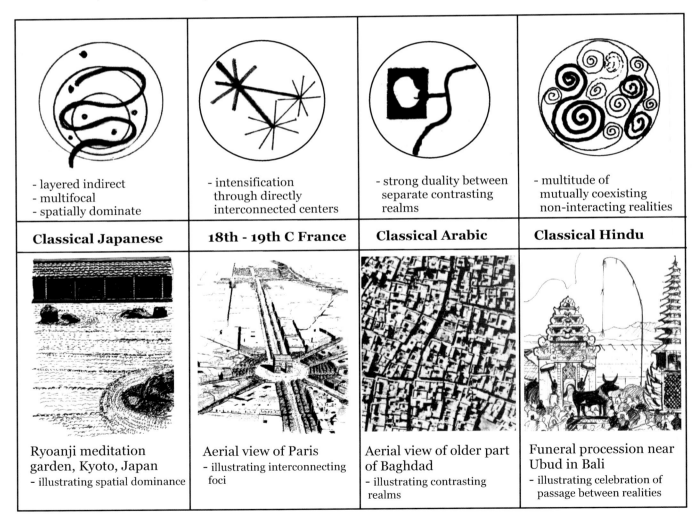

- layered indirect - multifocal - spatially dominate	- intensification through directly interconnected centers	- strong duality between separate contrasting realms	- multitude of mutually coexisting non-interacting realities
Classical Japanese	**18th - 19th C France**	**Classical Arabic**	**Classical Hindu**
Ryoanji meditation garden, Kyoto, Japan - illustrating spatial dominance	Aerial view of Paris - illustrating interconnecting foci	Aerial view of older part of Baghdad - illustrating contrasting realms	Funeral procession near Ubud in Bali - illustrating celebration of passage between realities

 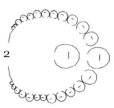 

Fractal generation of Ba-ila simulation (see page 26).
(*African Fractals* [62])

Ba-ila in Southern Zambia, 1920s.[63]

A classic sub-Saharan settlement pattern based on cattle husbandry. It consists of "Kraals" for protecting livestock at night, houses and storage structures. Gradation of wealth is expressed in the size of the extended family "Kraals," huts and location. Preferred areas are to the west, facing the rising sun and away from the entry gates. The Chief's complex is toward the center.

Although the cultural dimension of place provides substance, richness and continuity, there are several things that can create problems. Cultural mobility can disperse a pattern far from its original physical environment so that it is no longer a good cultural and ecological fit in its changed setting. Problems can also occur if some aspect of the cultural pattern becomes so fixed or extreme that it institutionalizes unintended consequences. Several examples of this occurred in traditional era 2 cultures.

  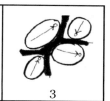

Illustration B-18 -- Examples of Dysfunctional Cultural Ecologies

1. In classical Hindu culture, separate social organizations froze into a caste system that became so ingrained that a large group outside of caste, the untouchables, became disenfranchised from society.

2. In the classical Arabic pattern, in its most recent puritanical form, the tradition of women taking the private realm of space into the public realm via clothing (the burka) has become so institutionalized that depersonalization of the feminine half of the population occurs outside the home.

3. The boundaries shown in the industrial diagram have, in many cases, become so severe as to eliminate any synergy that could exist between parts, reducing the efficiency that the culture prides itself on.

The irony of these three examples is that by becoming overly rigid, they produce the opposite of the original intention. Non-interaction among socially diverse peoples condemns a large group to a level of minimal existence, protection of women ends up oppressing women, and in the industrial society that is founded on the idea of efficiency, inefficiency is created by eliminating the potentials for synergistic relationships that could occur between parts.

[62] Ron Eglash, *African Fractals: Modern Computing and Indigenous Design.* Rutgers University Press, 1999.
[63] Bernard Rudofsky, *Architecture without Architects: A Short Introduction to Non-Pedigreed Architecture.* University of New Mexico Press, 1980.

- self-similar forms repeating through multiple scales	- dynamic pluralistic specialized segregated concentrations
Sub-Saharan Africa	**Classical Industrial**

Labbezanga in Mali - illustrating self-similar forms at multiple scales	Central Los Angeles in the mid-1980s

-- Patterns of Cultural Ecologies

The Inner Ecology: The Ecology of Soul and Spirit. Place has an inner dimension as well as a physical and cultural one. This dimension manifests itself in the often mysterious world of our subconscious. History reminds us of the infinite number of metaphorical forms the subconscious can take, with its gods and goddesses, demons and devils, saints and bodhisattvas, totemic animals and allies, prophets and mystics. Freud, Jung and many others helped reveal this inner aspect of place for Western society at the early part of the last century. The development of psychiatry argued that this layer of consciousness plays a large role in our perceptions, behavior and choices. Problems can occur if the inner subconscious ecology is in conflict with our physical and cultural ecology, since all three—physical place, cultural place and inner place—are connected in each individual. For a quality life each concept must be healthy since each influences the others to produce wholeness or fragmentation, health or neurosis. The history of the 20th century illustrates how destructive this type of fragmentation and neurosis can become.

Like our planetary ecology, which contains smaller patterns called biomes, our inner ecology also has a particular subset of environments. These include:

- The realm of emotions and feeling, which often act independently of rational thought.
- The realm of fantasy and imagination, which can be both creative and destructive.
- The dream world, which we may enter any night during sleep or during the day via daydreams.
- The realm of the shadow, where we attempt to exile from consciousness aspects we wish to deny.
- The collective unconscious—universal patterns, culturally derived and socially shared.

There are also inhabitants in this inner ecology. Carl Jung developed new terms to describe them. *Archetype* was used to describe universal figures that act out in our inner world, at times exerting tremendous influence of which we are seldom conscious. The concept of *animus* and *anima* describes the dance of the masculine and feminine sides of ourselves, and *shadow* describes dark figures that hide in our denial but still exert great influence and creativity.

Communication with this inner world employs a language that is composed of symbol and metaphor and emphasizes integration rather than differentiation. It is a language dominated by feeling rather than thinking. Joseph Campbell found this language to be the basis much of the rich folklore of humankind's myths,[64, 65] and Jung made use of it in dream analysis and methods for inner dialogue.[66, 67]

The illustrations on the next page are from art used to explore and communicate with the inner ecology. The subjects originate from dreams and are explored through painting and poetry.

---

[64] Joseph Campbell, *Transformations of Myth through Time.* New York: Harper Collins, 1990.
[65] Diane Osbon, *The Joseph Campbell Companion.* New York: Harper Perennial, 1992.
[66] Carl Jung, *Archetypes of the Collective Unconscious.* New York: Pantheon Books, 1959.
[67] Robert Johnson, *Innerwork.* San Francisco: Harpers, 1986.

Dark Mother Speaks

I am the container
for conscious walking birth.

To give birth to yourself spiritually
you must enter my dark cave,

confronting ghosts as you descend
dancing, stumbling, crawling, sliding,

down, down, bruised, kneaded,
through the birth canal of stone

until you are born, an adult standing,
ready to cross over the bridge,

to enter *new waters of consciousness,*
to rest there a time, before
surfacing in a pool of stars.

Totem Temple

From the barren desert sands
of ignorance and error
a temple filled with riches
reaches for the sky
a temple whose totems
are carved in your soul
a temple whose totems
sing of your wholeness.

...you must enter
you must explore its spacious
rooms and passageways
its hidden nooks and niches.
In its silent sanctuary
you must dwell with your ally
until temple and ally
dwell in you.

**<u>Illustration B-19 -- Dream Paintings by
Beverly Young</u>** [68]

Images tend to fall into a natural spectrum in degree of abstraction. **Picture** is at one end. In its purest form it is a replication of visual reality perceived by the conscious nervous system.

In the middle is the **diagram** which is best at describing the realities of processes. At the other end of the spectrum is the **symbol** which contains emotional reality.

Paintings based on meaning, not merely interesting exercises, must work the boundaries and interfaces of all three of these.

But beyond in the subconscious there is another self-similar layer consisting of **dreams, feelings, and archetypes.**

[68] Paintings by B. Young, Poetry by J. Elsdon. From *The Living Dream* by Beverly Young & Jane Elsdon, E & J Publishing, 1997.

B.2 Place
c. Planetary Dynamics

The unfolding story of plate tectonics and continental drift illustrates how dynamic the Earth is. We seem to be in a cyclic process of continental clustering and separation. As shown here, we now know this is more than just the progression from a super continent to the present seven continents. We started with a super continent (Rodina) that evolved to separate continents, then came together again in another super continent (Pangaea), and then separated again to become our present condition. North America has been the most mobile of the continents, having collided with South America, Northern Europe and Antarctica in its travels.[69]

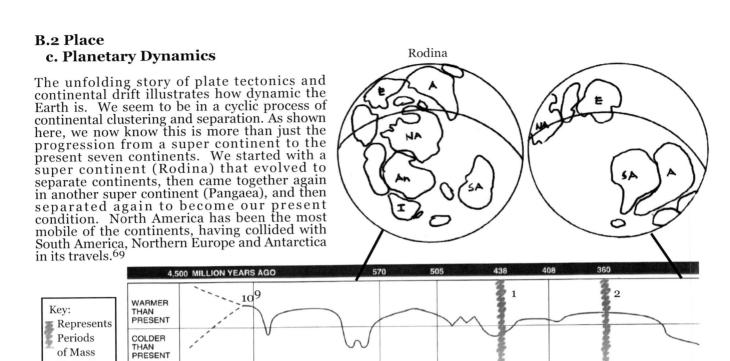

Illustration B-20 -- Relative temperature variations, phases of continental drift, and periods of mass extinction throughout Earth's history

This chart shows the relationship between the evolution of different life forms, changing climatic conditions and periods of mass extinction. Since time on this chart is plotted logarithmically, the right end is far more detailed than the left end. Recent studies indicate that most of the five large-scale periods of extinction were the result of catastrophic impacts from comets or asteroids. The statistical pattern of impact from a range of different sized extraterrestrial objects on the Earth is shown in the chart below.[70]

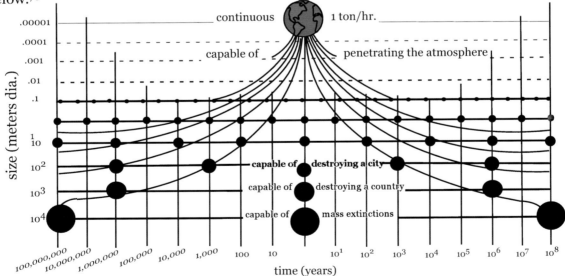

Illustration B-21 -- Statistical occurrences of extraterrestrial strikes on Earth

69 Ian Dalziel "Earth before Pangea." *Scientific American* (January 1993) 272:(1): 58-63.

70 C. Allegre and S. Schneider "The Evolution of the Earth." *Scientific American* (October 1994) 271: 44-51.

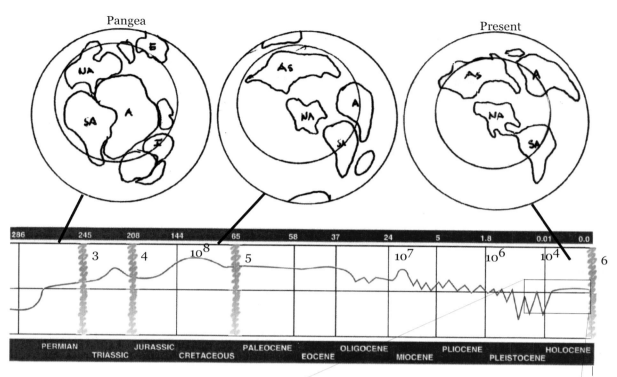

Evidence suggests that a sixth period of mass extinction is happening now--not the result of comets or asteroids, but of human effects on the planetary environment.[71] This points to the urgent need for us to become more coherent and sophisticated in our relationship to the planet. Environmental design must be part of a program that allows humankind to become a more positive and less destructive part of our place, the Earth.

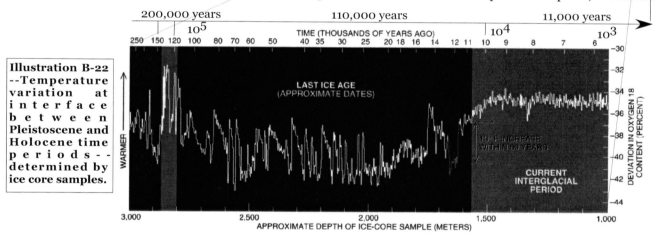

Illustration B-22 --Temperature variation at interface between Pleistoscene and Holocene time periods-- determined by ice core samples.

Measurements taken at different layers of the Greenland Ice Sheet have allowed scientists to plot temperature fluctuations over the last ice age, as shown in Illustration B-22.[72] While demonstrating the pattern of fluctuation over a 120,000 year period, it also reveals how quickly climate can shift. An example is a 13°F change in 50 years that occurred about 11,000 years ago, shown in red. We should be much less cavalier about human tinkering with complex chaotic environments. For example, our present global warming problem has been created by greenhouse gases from our over-reliance on fossil fuels. We live in ever-changing, dancing, chaotic systems. We are finally becoming aware of this. Now we need to design appropriately to become a creative part of these systems.

---

[71] Tom Gehrels, "Collision with Comets and Asteroids." *Scientific American* (March 1994), 90.

[72] W. Calvin, "The Emergence of Intelligence." *Scientific American* (October 1994), 101-107.

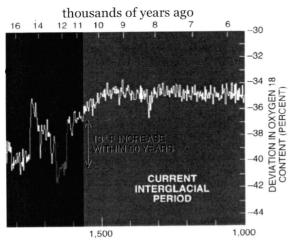

thousands of years ago

13° F INCREASE WITHIN 50 YEARS

CURRENT INTERGLACIAL PERIOD

DEVIATION IN OXYGEN 18 CONTENT (PERCENT)

Illustration B-23 -- Indictator of the rapid shift to a mild interglacial area in ice samples

The last ice age was beneficial for ocean life.[73] The cold ocean held nitrates, a key material for increased levels of the plankton that are fundamental to the ocean food chain. Carbon dioxide (CO_2) levels in the atmosphere dropped during this period as increased plankton soaked up CO_2.

The record of climate change preserved in the Greenland Ice Sheet indicates that the shift from hunting and gathering to agriculture and husbandry was as much a response to climate change as it was due to the stress from over-hunting and human ingenuity. The era of agriculture and husbandry coincides with the relatively mild interglacial era we are currently in, and that we are accentuating through human activity.

Illustration B-24 -- Massive flood scars in eastern Washington State, USA

Hunting and gathering of marine resources was evidently a greater part of the classical hunting and gathering era than first assumed. Large grazing mammals also did well in the outer edge of the glaciated areas. North America contained a large sub-arctic version of the Serengeti plains, complete with mammoths, giant sloths, large bison and saber-toothed tigers. Similar megafauna existed in Europe, Asia and Australia as well.

Massive temperature fluctuations during this period indicate how quickly changes can occur in the climate system. Evidence of some of these changes can be found in the natural history of eastern Washington State in the United States shown in Illustration B-24. In this area, we find scars that are the result of flooding on a scale almost impossible to imagine. Analysis of this ancient flood was part of the undoing of the theory of Uniformitarianism, the theory that change on the earth was always very slow and gradual, which had dominated the geological sciences until the 1940s.[74] This flood was found to be the result of the breaking of a glacial dam, and created a huge lake in what is now Idaho and Montana--Glacial Lake, Missoula. The catastrophic failure of this ice dam released 500 cubic miles of water into the Pacific Ocean in six days. The flow at the height of this flood was sixty times that of the Amazon River. Further analysis revealed that floods of this magnitude occurred several hundred times in this area as the ice dam repeatedly developed and failed. There are indicators of similar catastrophic floods into the Atlantic on the eastern edge of the North American continent. A comparable flood occurred in Asia Minor at the Bosporus about 8,000 years ago.[75] Major environmental events such as these can modify ocean currents and cause rapid climate changes.[76]

73 Richard Monastersky, "Ocean Life in the Ice Age: Time to Party." *Science News* (Sept. 2, 1995), 48.

74 Michael Parfit, "The Floods That Carved the West." *Smithsonian* (April. 1995), 48-58.

75 Rick Gore, "Wrath of the Gods: A History Forged by Disaster," *National Geographic* (July 2000), 52-71.

76 William F. Ruddiman, "How Did Humans First Alter Global Climate?" *Scientific American* (March 2005), 46-53.
    Some evidence exists that the beginning of the current interglacial period is a result of early agricultural patterns.

The Dynamics of Inner Ecology

Changes in philosophies and religions dance along with changes in physical and cultural ecology. The rise and fall of religions can also be looked at in the fractal view of time used earlier. Of particular interest for our situation today are periods of rapid synthesis of new cultural eras indicated on the steep part of the curves shown.

Illustration B-25 -- Fractal view of human population growth over time

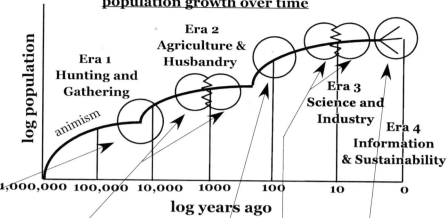

Era 1 Hunting and Gathering

Era 2 Agriculture & Husbandry

animism

Era 3 Science and Industry

Era 4 Information & Sustainability

log population

1,000,000 100,000 10,000 1000 100 10 0

log years ago

The Goddess religions of Northern Europe, the Mediterranean basin and the Middle East seem to be connected to the great neolithic inventions and cultural shift from era 1 to era 2.

Goddess statue of Catal Huyuk Analulia 5750 B.C.

Goddess statue from Megalithic temple in Malta, 3600 B.C.

Snake Goddess from Knossosia, Crete 1600 B.C.

Once developed, era 2 allowed vast concentrations of wealth and power and the inventions of empires, accompanied by a shift to patriarchal religions. Eventual reactions to raw power and violence resulted in peace-oriented philosophies and religions like Akhenaten's heracy, Taoism, Buddhism and early Christianity.

Akhenaten 1370 B.C.
Rameses II 1250 B.C.

Power and patriarchal emphasis was reasserted in Confusionism, Brahmanism, later Christianity and Islam.

Emphasis on knowledge, reason and practicality set the stage for the shift to era 3. This cultural era of Science and Industry allowed phenomenal physical development and freedom with an emphasis on the secular. Intense specialization and fragmentation weakened the sacred side of inner ecology.

Reaction to the disassociation from emotion, mass commercialism and disenfranchisement of certain groups resulted in a severe fundamentalist version of established religions. The clash of secularism and fundamentalism reflects and adds to the stress that always occurs at the end of each cultural era.

What will be the inner ecological response to the evolution of the new cultural era of information and sustainability? Interest in Buddhism in the West, revival of suppressed indigenous religions of Europe and Native American cultures and new connections like Deep Ecology are indicators of a search in progress.

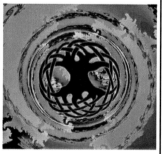

This search will ultimately evolve into an inner ecological belief more suited to our times, our knowledge, and our cultural conditions. As pointed out by Joseph Campbell, this can't be forced, but must evolve out of our unique situation.

B.2 Place
d. Aesthetics of place

Introduction. Section **A.1. d** reviewed some basic elements of aesthetics and implications for design from the concept of sustainability. In this context, aesthetics provides feedback regarding the health of an evolutionary system. Section **A.2. d** explored the relationship of fractal geometry and deterministic chaos to aesthetics. Here we found that complexity is essential to aesthetics rather than something to be feared and avoided. Section **B.1. d** discussed aesthetics as part of cultural dynamics, including how important cultural symbolism has been during historical shifts and changes. Place is where all of these aspects of aesthetics are applied.

Emphasis. The most recent movements in environmental design, Modernism and Postmodernism, each had an agenda with regard to aesthetics of place. The Modernist context of a scientific/industrial culture with an emphasis on use and function perceived nature as a resource to be exploited. With a few brilliant exceptions, Modernist aesthetic theories resulted in the homogenization of a "sense of place." Variety and intensity were reduced and regional differences minimized, creating architectural monocultures.

In contrast, the Post-Modern response attempted to intensify a sense of place by creating a place for events—a stage set. Function and historic consistency were placed in subordinate positions to the main concerns of intensity and drama, often derived from a vague classical European context. Literary elements such as allegory and metaphor were prominent design strategies. Both Modernist and Post-Modern approaches tended to be dominated by self-contained concepts and often resulted in exclusiveness and self-righteousness.

Aesthetic theory based on sustainability recognizes the validity of both of these approaches as interesting abstractions, but also recognizes that these abstractions are different symptoms of the same problem—fragmentation. When viewed from outside their own philosophical constructs, this fragmentation breaks the whole harmonic system of nature into dysfunctional and disconnected pieces.

For a sustainable future, a larger and broader ecological perspective will give priority to integration rather than differentiation in the design of place. Design will be perceived as a part of the healing of the earth; healing the amputations caused by thoughtless human activity or perceived "necessity." From the position of sustainable design, each place is unique yet connected to a harmonious and dynamic whole. Every place, in fact any part of the earth, is both unique and connected. These relationships are not linear and cannot be totally defined by abstractions, as useful as abstractions are. By transcending the perceived oppositions exemplified by Modernist and Post-Modernist theories, we can begin to help heal the earth through the sustainable design of place.

Climatically responsive design and passive solar applications are a start in this direction. They illustrate how, in healing the split between the technical and aesthetic aspects of environmental design, we can also heal our relationship to the natural processes of the Earth.

The aesthetic requirements of place expand the traditional aesthetic concerns of proportion, harmony and scale to include reunification of what has become fragmented and reconnection to a larger purpose. This needs to be done at a fractal order of scales, from the planet to the individual, from the setting to the specific materials. These concerns must be seen as components of a fractal series of wholes to be used in compositions that provide connection. Beauty, for instance, is not just in the eye of the beholder, or only expressed in formal composition. It is far more. The larger purpose of beauty is to provide critical feedback about whether a place is a contributor or a detriment to planetary, cultural, social, economic, community and individualized health and wholeness. For people totally immersed in the industrial-era values of separation and monocultural fragmentation, holistic reconnection seems impossible. But a small step outside this narrow mental constraint reveals the immense potential inherent in attending to wholeness and health at many levels—ecological, physical, aesthetic and economic.

Compositional techniques. In the environmental design disciplines, geometry is a major tool for dealing with aesthetics. A shift in geometric framework is one of the keys to evolution from an industrial to a sustainable culture. Therefore, we added another section to the previous chart comparing the characteristics of Euclidean to fractal geometry. This new section of the chart compares the aesthetic implications of these two geometries.

ABOUT	Euclidean Geometry	Fractal Geometry
11. **harmony**	Harmony can be achieved by simplification.	Harmony can be achieved by complexity.
12. **order & dynamics**	Control is an essential part of aesthetics.	Dancing with chaos is an essential part of aesthetics.
13. **symmetry**	Symmetry and asymmetry are important aesthetic devices.	Self-similarity and affine similarity are also important aesthetic devices.
14. **form expression**	Geometrical solids are the basic building blocks of aesthetics because it deals with differentiation.	Fluidity is an essential part of aesthetics because it deals with connectivity and process.

Illustration B-26 -- Extending Illustration A-17 (page 71) to include aesthetics

Place, time and health. These are the essential triad of an aesthetic system based on fractal and sustainable concepts. Clarity, feeling and synergy between these elements must be included in design decisions. The advantage of aesthetic systems is that, once mastered, they become intuitive, and evaluation becomes almost instantaneous.

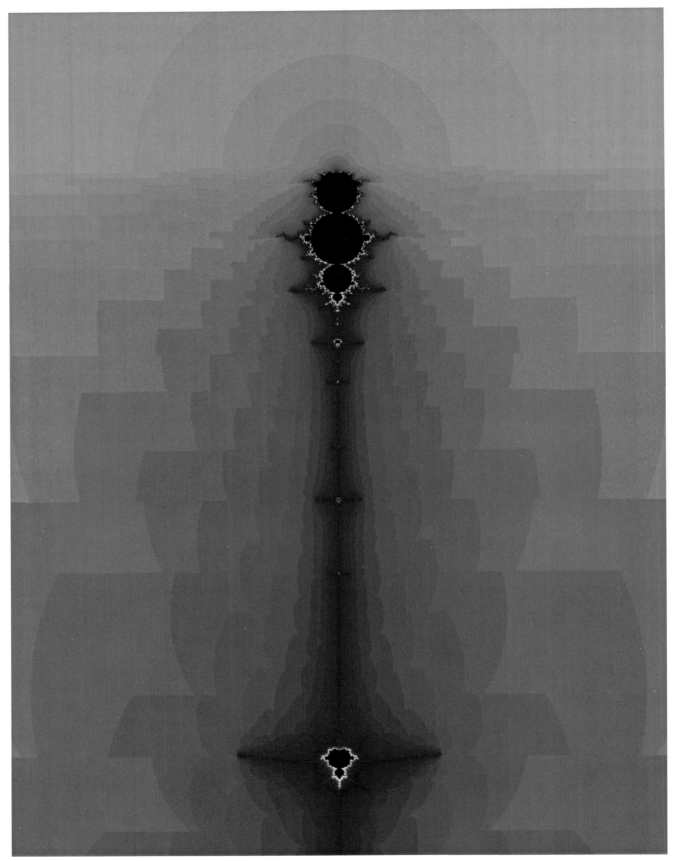

The computer generated fractal image on the preceding page illustrates:

1. Harmony
Harmony is coupled with a high degree of complexity.
Infinite complexity: One can zoom in forever and the resulting form will always be different though connected.

2. Order
This order is chaotic in nature.
The form of this fractal is replicable but not predictable.

3. Symmetry
Symmetry is composed of a mix of forms with self-similar and affine similarities.
This mix of symmetrical and asymmetrical forms occurs at an infinite number of scales.

4. Form
The form exhibits a high degree of fluidity as well as being composed of geometrical shapes.
All the forms generated in the image and background are strongly connected.

Fractals of this sort are like natural objects in that, while some are more interesting than others and some are more beautiful than others, none are really unattractive. This is generally true for most vernacular architecture in contrast to industrial-era architecture where ugliness is well-represented. The reason for this is because vernacular architecture is generated through a process involving multiple iterations, while most industrial architecture is developed in a process-light, abstraction-heavy context. Why can't human-made structures be as universally beautiful as natural landscapes? They can be if the rules of aesthetics are applied in a fractal manner and they become an integral part of the regenerative processes of the Earth.

In this way, context and time take on much greater meaning than in industrial-era architectural theory. A building can be thought of as a ship sailing a landscape ocean. This ocean can be a city, a town, a suburb or a rural setting, but this ship will adjust to optimize its relationship to the context. The seasons, the light, the sounds and the smells all are part of the total ocean in which this architectural ship sails.

B.2. Place
e. Life-cycle and regenerative design

Introduction. Exploration of place in the context of today's knowledge reveals the dynamic intersecting ecologies described. Such a look also revealed that, as a species, we are an integral part of the planetary ecology, for better or for worse. Sustainable design of place is based on the belief that we can affect planetary ecology for the better. Life-cycle and regenerative design are important techniques for making this happen.

Life-cycle design. The concept of life-cycle design is simple, but the result is revolutionary in the passing Era 3 context, and evolutionary in the developing Era 4. This technique is revolutionary in that it involves the merger of preconceived opposites in terms of industrial-era concepts: The merger of ecology and economy. Once we realize these are not necessarily in conflict, but instead are aspects of life that we separate at our peril, life-cycle design in various forms becomes available to us. Life-cycle design also illustrates why information and sustainability are integrally linked in this new era.

Life-cycle design is based on the idea that *all costs* and *benefits* over the life span of an asset or object need to be seriously considered. Costs to make, build or sell something we describe as *internal costs*. These costs are based on a linear single-use flow of materials and energy. These are only partial costs. The real costs, or *true costs*, involve these costs plus costs to the future, to social health, the environment and the planet. These additional costs are just as important and potentially as measurable as internal costs. True costs are developed by looking at the flow of materials and energy as cyclic rather than linear.

Once this relationship is accepted, life-cycle concepts can be developed that not only deal with cost, but can also take into consideration value. We must examine what good an asset can contribute with regard to social health, the environment and the planet. This shift allows the vast potential of synergy to occur in the process. This final step moves life-cycle assessment beyond accounting negative effects and regulation to optimization via life-cycle design. This requires a synthesis of information beyond classic industrial-era knowledge, which is now possible in our information-oriented culture. This approach is a key part in the cultural shift from Era 3 to Era 4.

However, the application of this idea is fraught with problems. The first is the degree of how hard or soft the data is concerning these different costs. Hard data implies concise, easily determined costs and benefits, and soft implies mushy, elusive data or uncertain effects. The cost of global warming, for example, has been estimated at $60 billion per year. But how accurate is this number? It is generally believed that internal costs are hard and precise. What could be more real than what you must actually pay out of pocket? With this mindset, other costs are more difficult to quantify and imbued with variable interpretations. However, some investigation reveals that even internal costs are not as hard as they appear. One of the reasons for this is the hidden subsidies that tilt the economic playing field. These subsidies are estimated to be about 10% for timber, 50% or more for water and as much as 90% for private automobile use. Costs are also critically affected by monetary and tax policies, and by incentives that are largely determined by fragmentary special interests.

Another problem is the degree of manipulation and large-scale inefficiencies that characterize the later stages of Era 3. A very clear recent example is the West Coast electrical energy crisis of 2001, when, after de-regulation in California, large energy producers were able to game the system to produce artificial scarcities, resulting in outrageous rate-hikes in the billions of dollars.

A look at internal costs and the true costs of electric energy production during this incident is very revealing regarding the increasingly artificial nature of internal costs.

Illustration B-27 -- Approximate costs of electricity (pre-deregulation in California)

	SOURCES:	a. Internal cost (¢/kw.hr)	b. True cost = internal + subsidies + environmental costs + health costs (¢/kw.hr)	c. Ratio: True cost/ Internal cost (a/b)
fossil fuels	coal	7	23+	2.6
	oil	7	20	2
	natural gas	6	14	2
traditional renewable	nuclear	10	22+	2+
	large hydro	4	14	3
	small hydro	6	9	1.6
	geothermal	7	9	1.3
newer renewable	biomass	8	10	1.25
	solar thermal	8	10	1.25
	wind	5	6	1.25
	photovoltaic	15	17	1.1
	green architecture includes passive solar heating & cooling, natural light and ventilation	2-5	0-3 We treat electricity saved by green design techniques as electricity produced that we would have to pay for without green design.	.6
	Cost to PG&E post de-regulation 2001	33	PG&E, once the largest private utility in the country, was in bankruptcy court as a result of this inefficiency of large scale.	

This data was collected by David Bainbridge, Professor of Sustainable Management at Alliant International University in San Diego, California, using data from the U.S. Department of Energy, the Council for Renewable Energy, the Responsible Investors Research Center and his own estimates of environmental costs.

Dividing the internal cost by the true cost provides the ratios listed in the third column. These ratios reveal the discrepancies between internal costs and true costs. One can argue with a few cents here and there, but it is the patterns illustrated by this chart that are important. The true-cost to internal-cost ratio is less for renewables and more renewables are becoming competitive with fossil fuels, even at the internal-cost level. Ironically, the three energy sources with the largest ratio of true-cost to internal-cost are the ones most heavily subsidized by the Federal government. This reveals that something is very wrong with regard to energy policies in North America.

Green architecture has one of the lowest internal costs and is the only energy source where the true costs are less than the internal costs. This is because of the synergy achieved by optimizing orientation, using recycled and "waste" products for materials (e.g., straw bales), and the health and productivity advantages of the resulting passive heating, cooling and natural lighting. In addition, green buildings use a minimum of government subsidies.

Determining true costs means accounting for the life cycle of the materials and energy used in buildings. Approaches to life cycle analysis and design and the complex information they require are in a state of rapid evolution. Listed below are terms and approaches currently in use.[77]

Life-Cycle Costing — A traditional engineering practice to calculate total cost of ownership over the life cycle of an asset. This is an internal cost financial tool with no environmental costs included.

Materials Life-Cycle Assessment — Analysis of the true costs of materials, including environmental costs used over the life-cycle of an asset.
(Also called "cradle to grave" analysis.)

Energy Life-Cycle Assessment — Analysis of the true cost of energy used over the life cycle of an asset.

Life-Cycle Assessment (LCA) — Analysis of total true cost of materials and energy over the life cycle of an asset.

14040 standards for Life-Cycle Assessments — To help refine these approaches and give some semblance of order to the complexities of LCAs the International organization for Standards has set forth LCA standards in their 14040 publications.

Problems with an item-by-item approach to LCAs are formidable. Much of the information needed is proprietary, and much of the data needed for life-cycle impacts is not yet well developed. The important thing, however, is that life-cycle analysis has begun on many fronts. What better problem to test and extend the capabilities of our information era?

In the meantime systems such as the LEED rating system, developed by the U.S. Green Building Council, are being used to evaluate green buildings from a qualitative perspective using a point system. As life-cycle analysis develops, this system, and others, will help provide a greater qualitative dimension to this effort.

At the other end of the spectrum from the step-by-step processes of life-cycle assessment are macro-scale approaches. These approaches use large scale models such as the U.S. Department of Commerce data on input-output flows for entire sectors of the economy. An example of an LCA using this approach is the "Baseline Green" tool developed by the Center for Maximum Potential Building Systems in conjunction with BNIM Architects. (See example on page 132.)

---

[77] Nadav Malin, "Life Cycle Assessment for Buildings, Seeking the Holy Grail." *Environmental Building News* II, #3 (March 2002).

Once we look holistically at the situation, beyond internal costs to consider true costs via life-cycle assessment, we can add design considerations to this analytical process. This allows us to consider value as well as costs. This optimization of the process extends the thinking of "cradle to grave" resource cycles to "cradle to cradle" cycles. This shift in design thinking allows enormous potential advantages for everyone as life-cycle design and triple bottom line accounting begin to be implemented at a large scale.

<u>Life-Cycle Design (LCD)</u>	A synthesis of analysis and design using life-cycle assessment that creates cradle to cradle resource cycles.
<u>Triple Bottom Line Accounting</u>	A term developed by British business consultant John Elkington in 1997 that refers to environmental, societal and financial accounting as one holistic package.

The advantages of this shift in design thinking are clearly articulated by Bill McDonough, a green architect, and Michael Braungart, an industrial chemist, who together have done life-cycle design for many industrial products and buildings.[78]

McDonough and Braungart developed a design tool to help achieve triple bottom line accounting for life-cycle design. It is based on our old fractal friend the Sierpinski gasket (see page 60). Each point of the triangle is one of the triple bottom line elements, and points between each illustrate the different combinations of points on each side. Being a fractal, there are infinite combinations possible, just as in human social behavior.

An important point made by this fractal diagram is that in a sustainably functioning system, all three points, as well as everything in between, are essential parts of a whole and need to be valued as such. "-Isms," which result from assuming one part is more important than the others, are destructive to the system. This was certainly the situation in the 20th century with the loss of millions of lives and vast resources due to conflicts between -isms. The 21st century must recognize that all three concerns and countless combinations thereof are symbiotic parts of a larger whole. Diversity is necessary for the health and stability of a system that works for everyone, including all species on Earth.

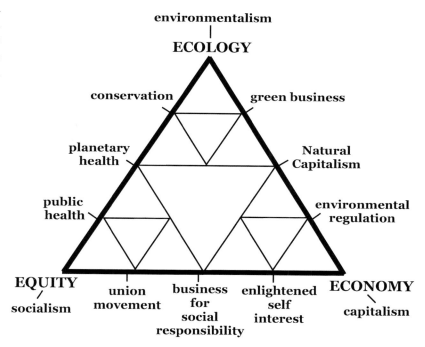

<u>Illustration B-28 -- Fractal illustration of diversity necessary for sustainable development</u>

78 William McDonough and Michael Braungart, *Cradle to Cradle*. New York: North Point Press, 2002.

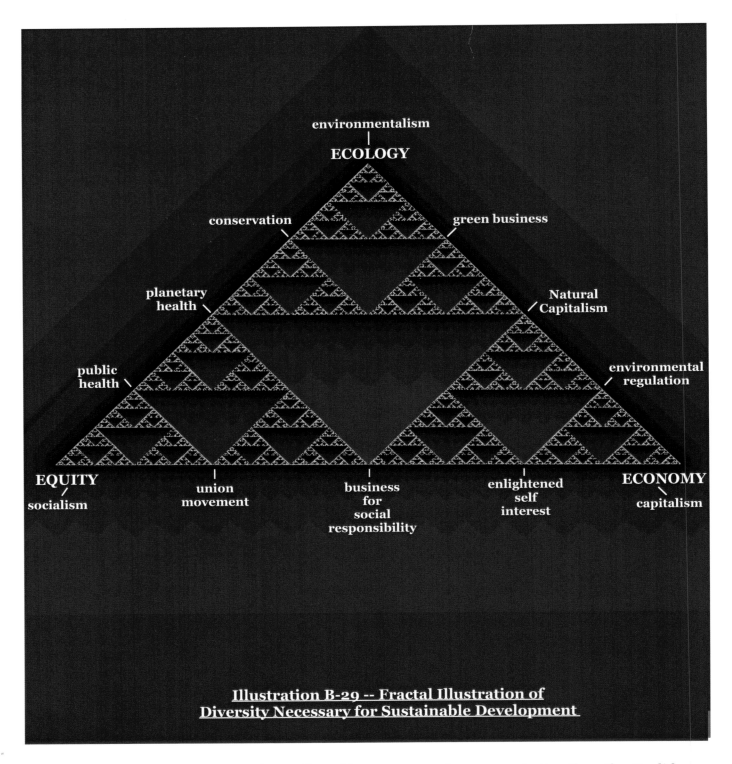

Illustration B-29 -- Fractal Illustration of Diversity Necessary for Sustainable Development

This fractal diagram expresses the reality of interconnected concerns better than the Euclidean triangle on the previous page because it shows the infinite variations possible between these three critical aspects of society: EQUITY, ECOLOGY and ECONOMY.

Rather than waiting for a perfect database for life-cycle analysis, some sustainable design groups are developing integrated design tools based on currently known life-cycle concepts. A good example of the application of life-cycle considerations to the design of place is the Eco-Balance Planning Game™ developed by the Center for Maximum Potential Building Systems in Austin, Texas. This planning and design tool combines the ecological footprint concepts of Wackernagle (see page 15) with life-cycle analysis and life-cycle design, to develop a process for in-depth place-oriented life-cycle optimization.

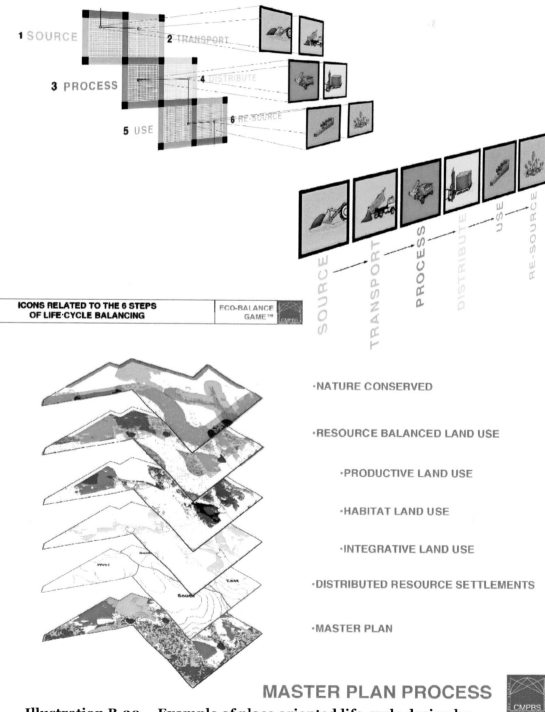

Illustration B-30 -- Example of place oriented life-cycle design by Center For Maximum Potential Building Systems

Regenerative design of places. In *Regenerative Design for Sustainable Development*, author John Lyle[79] describes environmental design as either part of a degenerative process that degrades the environment, or part of a regenerative process that helps maintain the environment. The impact of Era 2 and Era 3 has been so great that a significant part of Era 4 design will be to regenerate degraded environments and landscapes while simultaneously providing for human activities and needs. This is similar to the relationship between life-cycle assessment and life-cycle optimization where the goal of doing 'less harm' is expanded to doing 'more good'.

To include landscape regeneration as part of sustainable design processes, we need to recognize again how dynamic natural environments really are. This is important in facilitating the modification of two mindsets that get in the way of a successful practice of regenerative design.

The first of these mindsets is the tendency to think of natural landscape as being in equilibrium outside of human effect. Accordingly, protection and continued stability are viewed as the goal. Federal policies in the United States with regard to fire prevention and flood protection are large-scale examples of this mindset, where flood and fire were assumed to be destructive natural disasters. However, we have recently discovered that some non-equilibrium is a critical aspect of the health of many ecosystems. Now federal policies are slowly being modified to create "controlled burns" in National Forests and Parks and controlled floods in some areas downstream from large dams. We are slowly coming to realize that the occasional disturbances we call "natural disasters" are an important part of the maintenance and operation of ecosystems and the resulting landscapes.[80]

This certainly does not mean continuous disturbances accomplished by degenerative design are desirable. Instead, it means that occasional disturbances are an essential part of the system. Examples include be fires, earthquakes and landslides in Mediterranean biomes; fires, floods and grazing by hoofed animals in grassland biomes; floods, droughts and tornadoes in the southwestern United States; hurricanes and typhoons in coastal subtropical and tropical areas.[81] Disturbance and regenerative processes are occurring constantly at multiple scales. We too must become a part of this dynamic process. We have to tune in to the specificity of place, and then design to be a regenerative, rather than degenerative force. We won't ever know everything that is involved. What is important is to hear the music and start to dance. With familiarity and practice, our steps will improve.

The second mental barrier to regenerative design is the general impression that the processes of natural regeneration are so slow that our participation is not very important, or will not occur in time to be appreciated. Some regenerative processes are slow, but many others are relatively rapid; faster than most people, including designers, generally realize. Many occur rapidly enough so that we can participate and see results in a fairly short period of time. Illustration B-31 shows the regenerative process over a six-year period of a landscape in central California that burned in a 40,000 acre fire in 1994. This "natural disaster" triggered a sequential succession from fire-following flowers, vines and small herbs, then grasses and low shrubs, followed by bigger shrubs, to mixed oak savannah and mature chaparral in six years.

79 John Tillman Lyle, *Regenerative Design for Sustainable Development*, Wiley Publishers, 1996.
80 Seth Reice, *The Silver Lining – The Benefits of Natural Disasters*, Princeton University Press, 2001.
81 Allan Savory and Jody Butterfield, *Holistic Management: A New Framework for Decision Making*, Island Press, 1999.

The building shown under construction two years after the fire was designed to be a part of the regenerative process of this dynamic landscape. Landscape regeneration will have to become an integral part of the design process in all forms of environmental design in a sustainable cultural era.

Not all landscapes are as dynamic as the illustration shown here, but all are important in the multiple layers of wholeness that landscape includes, from the individual plant to the entire planet. This means the design of any project needs to be attuned to the whole system, including solar energy, water flows, wind patterns, plant communities and maintenance processes that relate to the particular place that we, as designers, call "the site."

Illustration B-31 -- Landscape regeneration over a six-year period following a wildfire

134

B.2. Place
f. Example: The Trout Farm complex

Introduction. Life-cycle and regenerative design applied to place is necessary in many settings, including regional, urban, town, suburban and rural. Some people argue that sustainable design, particularly architecture, should be strictly concentrated in existing built-up areas, leaving more rural areas intact. It is true that our urban areas need a great deal of attention, and the distinction between urban and rural places should be maintained and strengthened. We need to recognize, however, that very few rural areas are pristine, intact and healthy. The industrialized mining, agriculture and recreational practices of Era 3 have impacted all rural places except, perhaps, those few designated as wilderness. Even these have been affected by climate change, acid rain and other pollutants. Therefore, sustainable design using life-cycle and regenerative principles needs to be applied almost everywhere. The differences are only in the specifics of landscape, relationship to density and infrastructure. Examples used in this book have included a small North American town, an isolated individual building, and an island settlement pattern with a very high density by present urban standards.

The final example—an architectural complex—is set in a rural canyon adjacent to a National Forest. To a casual observer it appears to be in a relatively pristine rural environment. In reality, however, the landscape that has endured strip mining, ore processing, charcoaling of oak trees for gunpowder manufacture, intense road and cabin site grading, motorcycle racing and human-exacerbated wildfires. It was a degraded landscape, but it has also benefited over the last 25 years from human occupation employing sustainable design techniques to restore health to this unique place.

Context. The site is located on the central coast of California, at the boundary between a coastal climate to the south and an inland climate to the north. A ridge separating these two climatic zones is high enough to wring rainfall out of the predominantly southwest storm fronts, yet not high enough to drop the majority of water on the windward side. Most of the rain is deposited on the leeward side at this site, where rainfall averages 32" a year. To the south rainfall averages 22" a year; 16 miles to the east it averages only 6" a year. This site is wetter than the regional norm and also colder and more shadowed because it its location on a steep north slope. Thus, more moisture is maintained than the local average during the long dry season from late spring through early winter in this Mediterranean biome.

Geology and soil type accentuate the edge condition characteristics of this site. The geology of the Cuesta Ridge, just south of the site, is serpentine. Serpentine soil is generated from off-shore trenches at the west edge of past subduction zones, the result of the Pacific plate diving under the North American plate. Over the past ten million years, these formations have been uplifted and become exposed in many parts of the Coast Ranges, making these some of the youngest mountain ranges on the continent. Serpentine soils are high in magnesium and iron but deficient in calcium, sodium and potassium. This means the area is not very productive for traditional agriculture; probably the main reason this ridge was included in the Los Padres National Forest. Serpentine formations often contain heavy metals such as nickel, cobalt, copper and chromium, accounting for the mining activity on the site early in the 20th century. Many plants cannot tolerate serpentine soils, but some can adapt. Sargent Cypress, Knob and Colter Pines, Manzanita, Chamise, Cuesta Ridge Checker Bloom and Soaproot Lilies do well.

Edge condition characteristics of the site are repeated in the gradation of soil type from the serpentine ridge to more fertile soil downgrade at Tassajara Creek. This can be easily seen by observing the native tree variation from the ridge to Tassajara Creek over the short distance contained on this site. Sargent Cypress dominates the ridgetop, where they form a bonsai-like dwarf forest due to shallow soil conditions. Halfway down the ridge, in riparian areas where the soils are deeper, these cypresses grow rather large—up to three feet in diameter. Cypress are fast-growing, do well in fire conditions, and make excellent lumber although they are not common enough to be a traditional lumber tree. Approaching Tassajara Creek to the north, the range of cypress ends, giving way to White Oak, which are quite common along Tassajara Creek and to the north and east but whose southern range ends at about the same point as the large cypress trees. White Oaks like deep soils and do not occur naturally on the ocean side of Cuesta Ridge, which is dominated by Live Oaks. Added to this diverse landscape are Tan Bark Oaks, several types of scrub oaks that hybridize easily and are thus extremely variable, and larger hybrids like Oracle Oak, which is a cross between Live Oak and Black Oak. Edge conditions of this site reflect the progressive miniaturization of landscape scale that can be seen going from the Great Plains westward to the Pacific coast, as shown in Illustration B-32.

These conditions and the intimately folded topography help create a unique microclimate of wonderful subtlety and power. For example, after nine dry months, when the grass is brown, just after all the oaks produce a surprisingly abundant supply of acorns in the best late-fall fashion, just as it is getting dark early, just as temperatures are dropping into the thirties and there will soon be a hard freeze, it rains and spring erupts. Billions of tiny seeds sprout in delicate green shoots in an overwhelming variety of forms. For these seeds the time has arrived in spite of increasing darkness and inevitable freezes to come. Billions of them gamble they will get big enough, or the freeze will be light enough, that they will survive. The race is on to use water while it is available. Who knows?—the rainy season may be short and skimpy. The eternal dance with chaos has just intensified. This is the spring within the winter. Another spring will come with the blooming of the chaparral in March, and another with late-blooming species like Soaproot in the heat of summer. In this place there is a sequence of springs sandwiched between bouts of cold that can include heavy snows every five years or so and heat that can reach as high as 112° Fahrenheit.

Fifteen years ago this sequence began in early January; now it begins in early December. This shift illustrates the immediacy of the problem of global warming. Collectively, we can slow this shift by taking up carbon dioxide through the regeneration of forests and by producing less greenhouse gasses in the way we live. Both of these are being done with sustainable design at this unique place we call the Trout Farm.

On the following pages we show how sustainable design for the Trout Farm evolved as an example of the use of design to participate in regeneration of the land and to create sustainable architecture. We hope other designers will join us in applying these concepts to their own opportunities for design, and thus help transform humanity's relationship to the Earth from destructive to benign.

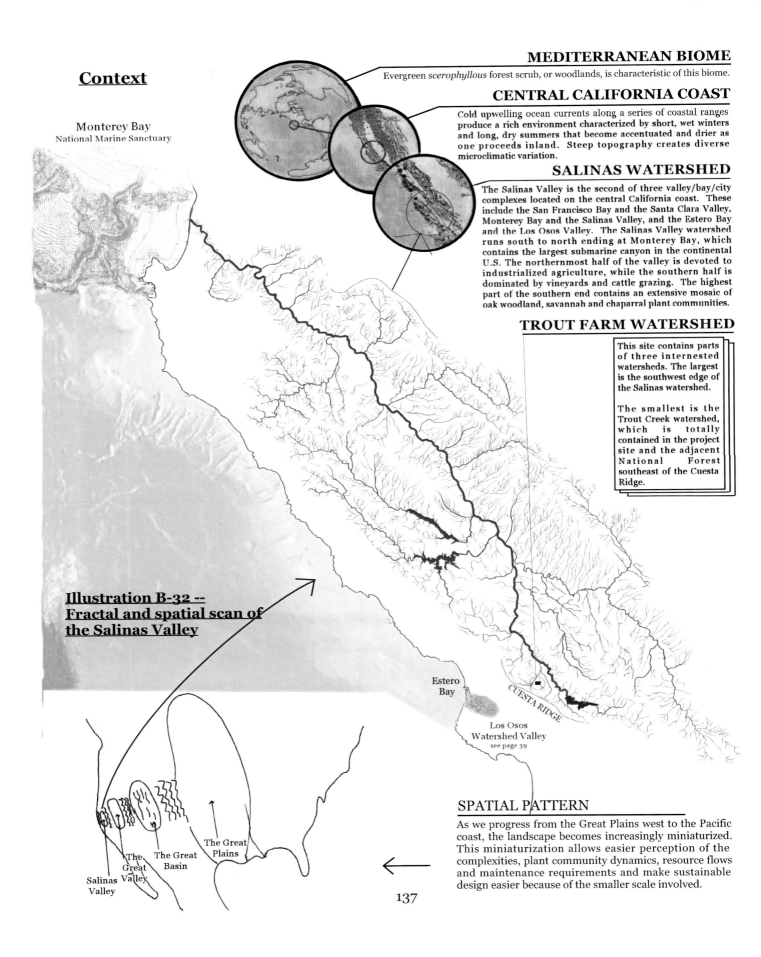

Context

Monterey Bay
National Marine Sanctuary

MEDITERRANEAN BIOME

Evergreen *scerophyllous* forest scrub, or woodlands, is characteristic of this biome.

CENTRAL CALIFORNIA COAST

Cold upwelling ocean currents along a series of coastal ranges produce a rich environment characterized by short, wet winters and long, dry summers that become accentuated and drier as one proceeds inland. Steep topography creates diverse microclimatic variation.

SALINAS WATERSHED

The Salinas Valley is the second of three valley/bay/city complexes located on the central California coast. These include the San Francisco Bay and the Santa Clara Valley, Monterey Bay and the Salinas Valley, and the Estero Bay and the Los Osos Valley. The Salinas Valley watershed runs south to north ending at Monterey Bay, which contains the largest submarine canyon in the continental U.S. The northernmost half of the valley is devoted to industrialized agriculture, while the southern half is dominated by vineyards and cattle grazing. The highest part of the southern end contains an extensive mosaic of oak woodland, savannah and chaparral plant communities.

TROUT FARM WATERSHED

This site contains parts of three internested watersheds. The largest is the southwest edge of the Salinas watershed.

The smallest is the Trout Creek watershed, which is totally contained in the project site and the adjacent National Forest southeast of the Cuesta Ridge.

**Illustration B-32 --
Fractal and spatial scan of
the Salinas Valley**

Estero
Bay

CUESTA RIDGE

Los Osos
Watershed Valley
see page 39

The Great
Plains

The Great
Plains

The Great Basin

The
Great Valley

Salinas
Valley

SPATIAL PATTERN

As we progress from the Great Plains west to the Pacific coast, the landscape becomes increasingly miniaturized. This miniaturization allows easier perception of the complexities, plant community dynamics, resource flows and maintenance requirements and make sustainable design easier because of the smaller scale involved.

137

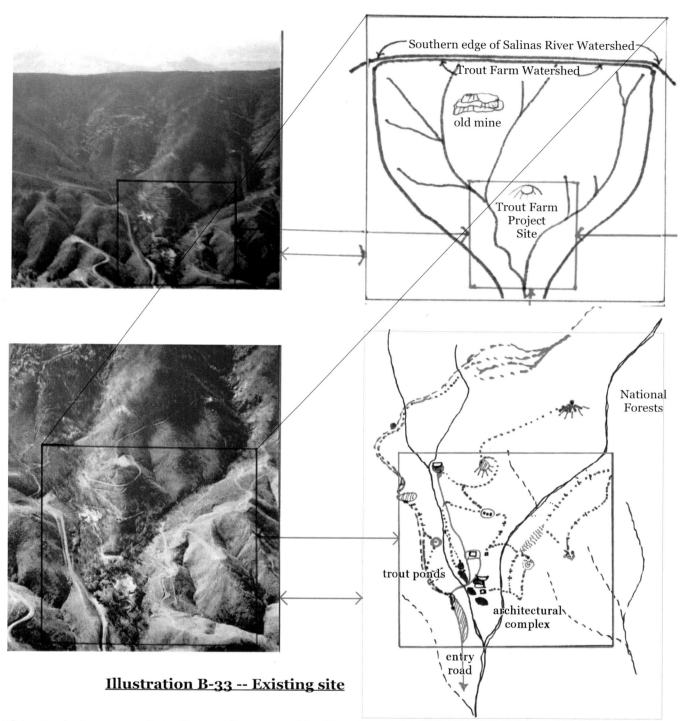

Illustration B-33 -- Existing site

This site design responds to the requirements of healing the site and the Trout Creek watershed from damage done from 1910 to 1979 by mining, grading and motorcycle racing. Sporadic wildfires are also a major design factor in this location. The aerial photographs above, taken after a fire in 1994, reveal mining and road scars on the site. Healing the watershed required controlling erosion caused by all these factors to the point where water flows were regenerative rather than degenerative. Infrastructure, energy production and materials used for construction were drawn from the existing conditions.

The architectural program for this site is for a mixed-use complex of research, offices, and residential facilities. The complex is designed to draw most of its energy for heating, cooling, lighting and electrical generation from the site by passive means. In addition, 80% of the wood used in construction of the buildings is obtained from the site, utilizing trees killed by the 1994 fire.

138

Site conditions. The site, located on a severe north slope, has relatively cold winters with the sun setting at 2:30 p.m. in December. Summers are hot and dry with temperatures occasionally reaching 112° Fahrenheit. Fire is a natural part of the ecology here, as it is for much of California. The winter wetness of this site accentuates this condition by the abundance of biomass it helps produce. The local plant communities have coevolved with fire for millions of years. The central challenge is that present human occupants (ourselves included) have yet to come to grips with the characteristics of this unique and beautiful ecological circumstance. Collective attempts to control fire have only lengthened the intervals between fire events and increased the level of destruction for each occurrence. From a sustainable viewpoint, each fire is just another iteration of many that will help us become a more integral part of this ecology, if we accept this feedback.

The site has many unique features including seven trout ponds and plantings developed in the early 1950s. Of particular interest are dwarf Sargent Cypress growing in the adjacent Los Padres National Forest, designated as a unique botanical preserve. Trees here average two inches in diameter, while the same trees around each creek in riparian areas can grow to three feet in diameter due to the more favorable soil conditions.

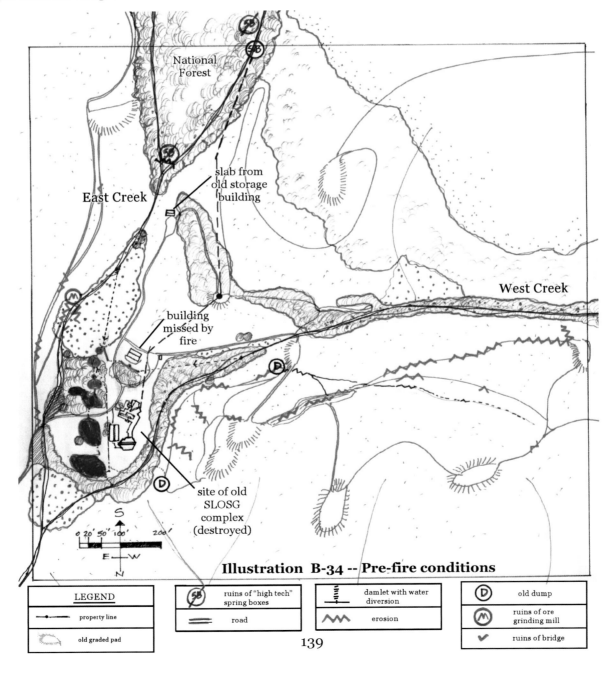

Illustration B-34 -- Pre-fire conditions

LEGEND			
	ruins of "high tech" spring boxes	damlet with water diversion	old dump
property line	road	erosion	ruins of ore grinding mill
old graded pad			ruins of bridge

139

The 40,000 acre wildfire that burned this area in August of 1994 was the stimulus for updating the infrastructure, assisting landscape regeneration, developing more appropriate sustainable buildings, instituting a continuing program of erosion control and healing many of the scars from previous industrial processes that had occurred on the site.

This activity gives as well as takes. The dead trees from the fire were milled on site, giving over 20,000 board feet of high quality custom lumber at a reasonable price. Regeneration of the landscape occurred in waves, starting with specialized fire-following plants like fire poppies, progressing through herbs and low shrubs to larger shrubs and brush to regeneration of the forests. In seven years, the landscape had regained much of its previous character.

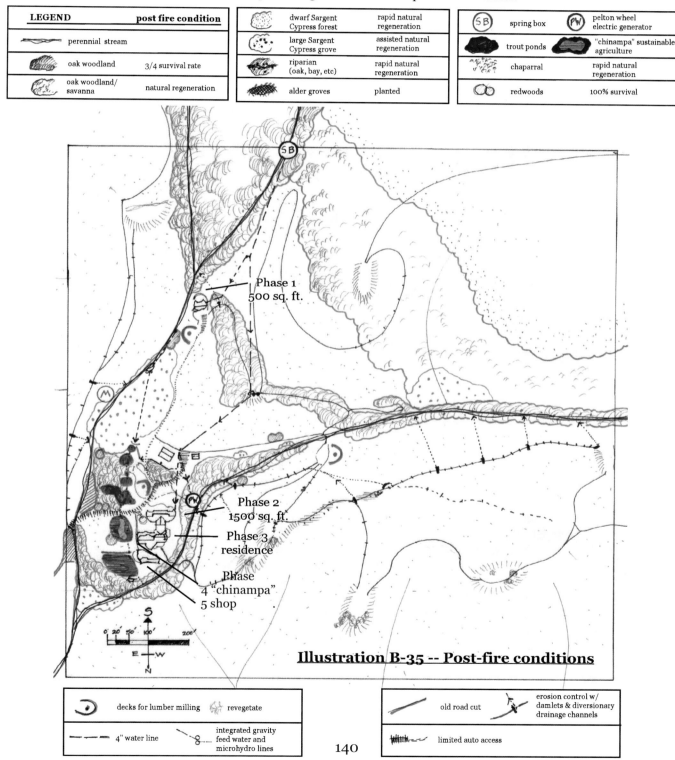

LEGEND	post fire condition
perennial stream	
oak woodland	3/4 survival rate
oak woodland/ savanna	natural regeneration

dwarf Sargent Cypress forest	rapid natural regeneration
large Sargent Cypress grove	assisted natural regeneration
riparian (oak, bay, etc)	rapid natural regeneration
alder groves	planted

SB spring box		PW	pelton wheel electric generator
trout ponds			"chinampa" sustainable agriculture
chaparral			rapid natural regeneration
redwoods			100% survival

Phase 1
500 sq. ft.

Phase 2
1500 sq. ft.

Phase 3
residence

Phase
4 "chinampa"
5 shop

Illustration B-35 -- Post-fire conditions

decks for lumber milling		revegetate	
4" water line		integrated gravity feed water and microhydro lines	

old road cut		erosion control w/ damlets & diversionary drainage channels
limited auto access		

140

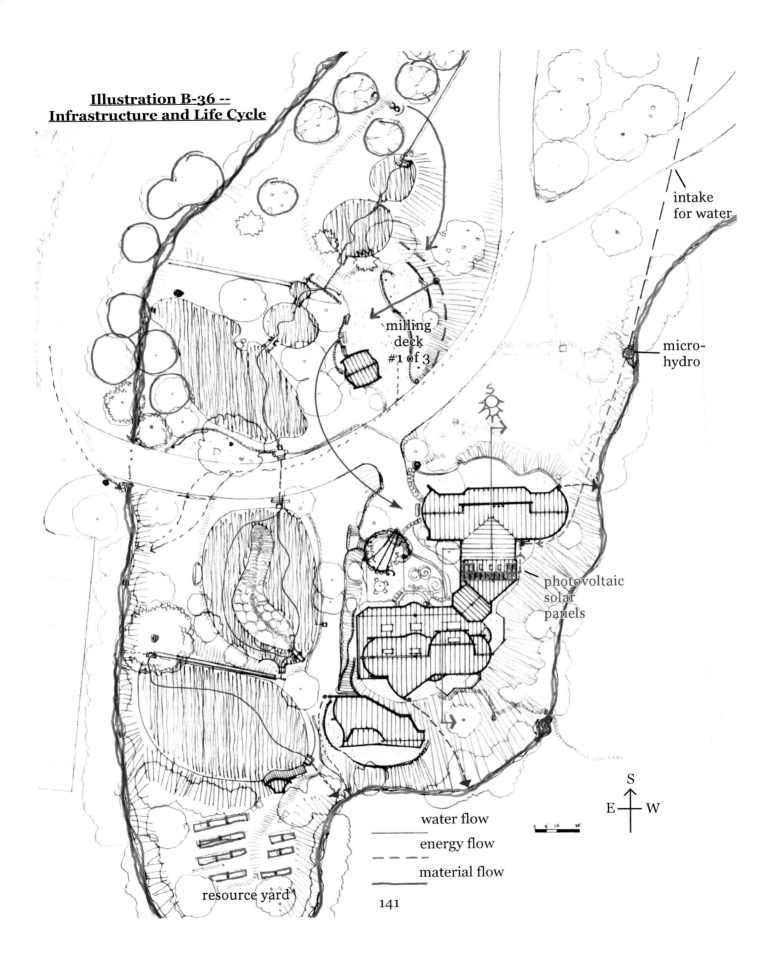

Illustration B-36 --
Infrastructure and Life Cycle

intake
for water

micro-
hydro

milling
deck
#1 of 3

photovoltaic
solar
panels

water flow

energy flow

material flow

S

E W

resource yard

141

Regeneration and life-cycle design

Approach. The goal was to integrate infrastructure and building reconstruction with the natural process of landscape regeneration. This required water flow, available materials and on-site energy production to be connected to develop the multiple benefits of synergy.

Red legged frogs in pond

Landscape regeneration. Most landscape regeneration is self-directing since native plants in this fire ecology have evolved to regenerate after a burn. Working in partnership with this process has advantages. For example, it is important that trees don't shade the building site to allow utilization of solar energy. In addition, keeping water flow optimized is critical to landscape regeneration, wildlife habitat, erosion control and back-up electricity production. The creeks are often chaotic due to the small size and steepness of this watershed. Early attempts to utilize the creeks didn't take this into account. This is illustrated by the ruins of high-tech spring boxes, water diversion devices to the ponds and a bridge to the old mill site. The broken concrete remains of these artifacts are testimony to the fact that it is better to use low-tech approaches that can be adjusted seasonally and be easily replaced when required.

Milling lumber from fire-killed trees

Material flows. Most of the lumber used in the reconstruction of the four buildings of the complex was obtained from trees killed in the fire and milled on site. Twenty-two thousand board feet of high quality lumber of mixed species was obtained, providing for construction needs plus a surplus stored in the resource yard just north of the lowest pond.

Straw bales were used for most exterior walls and some ceilings, garden walls, and outdoor benches. The interior stuccoed skin of these walls provides thermal mass for passive heating and cooling as well as allowing non-Euclidean form. Burned metal siding, broken concrete, and aluminum from the fire were used as siding, erosion control and ornamentation.

Microhydro power unit

Energy flows. Natural lighting, passive solar heating and cooling, natural ventilation, energy efficient appliances and on-site electricity production using sun and water provide a power grid-free complex. The result is a complex free of utility bills and lines, market manipulations, and the larger environmental consequences of electricity production. A pleasant side effect is that operating the system allows the occupants to participate in the chaotic dance of sun, water, vegetation and material flows which helps us appreciate and maintain the whole system.

Fire art--burned metal from 1994 fire

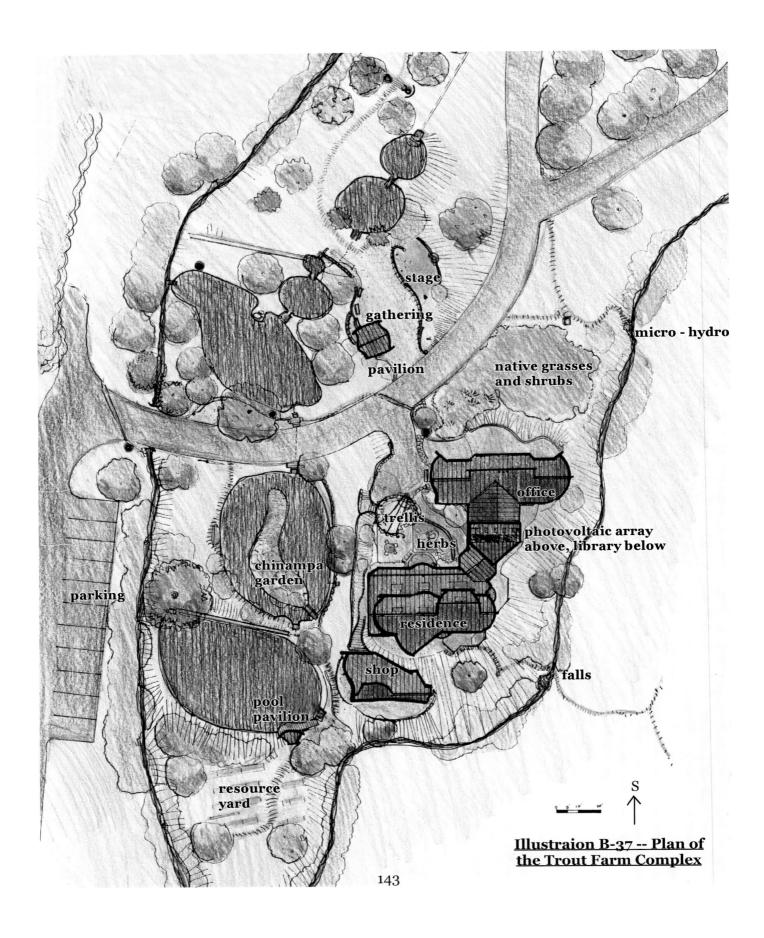

stage

gathering

pavilion

micro - hydro

native grasses
and shrubs

office

photovoltaic array
above, library below

trellis

herbs

chinampa
garden

parking

residence

shop

falls

pool
pavilion

resource
yard

S

<u>Illustraion B-37 -- Plan of
the Trout Farm Complex</u>

LEGEND

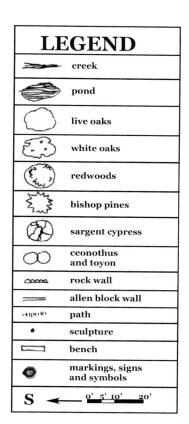

Symbol	Description
	creek
	pond
	live oaks
	white oaks
	redwoods
	bishop pines
	sargent cypress
	ceonothus and toyon
	rock wall
	allen block wall
	path
	sculpture
	bench
	markings, signs and symbols

S ← 0' 5' 10' 20'

TROUT FARM COMPLEX

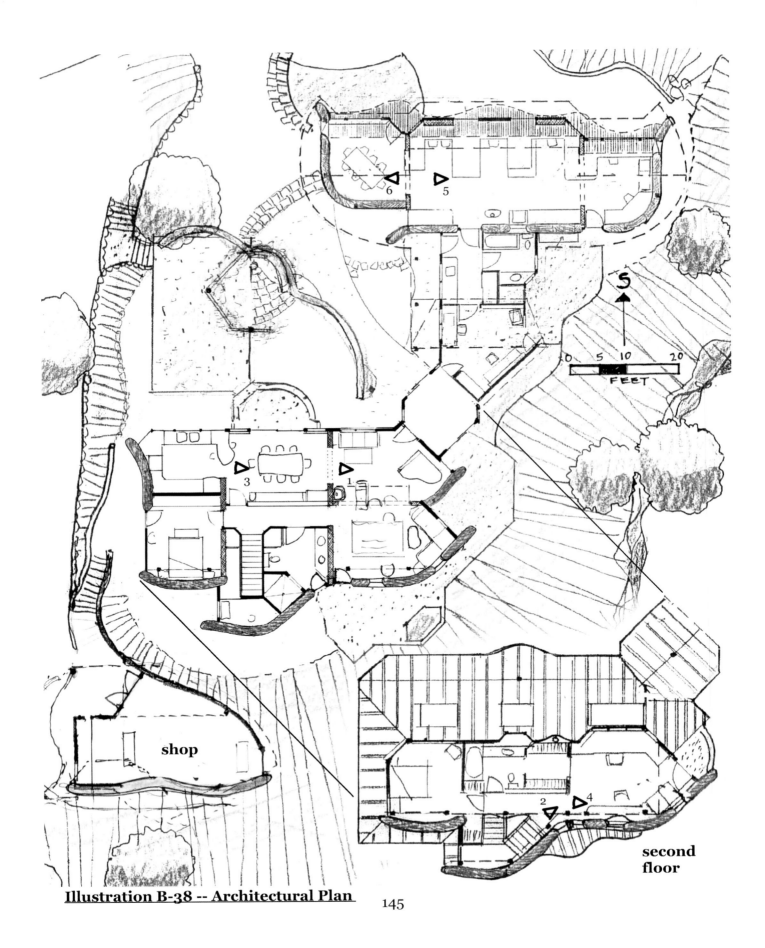

shop

second
floor

Illustration B-38 -- Architectural Plan

145

$\triangledown$ 1

$\triangledown$ 2

$\triangledown$ 3

$\triangle$ 4

$\triangleleft$ 5

$\triangle$ 6

Aesthetics. Fractal geometry allows a better understanding of the natural processes of iteration and feedback that are keys to co-designing with complexity and beauty. This allows the architecture to better relate to its setting through self-similarity and affine similarity at a series of connected scales.

Building generated as landscape is regenerated.

Fractal geometry also gives us a new way to use the universal elements of aesthetics:

> **harmony**
> **proportion**
> **scale**
> **sequence**
> **rhythm**
> **order**
> **form**
> **theme**
> **clarity**
> **synergy**

to produce complexity and diversity.

Two years later--both grown in.

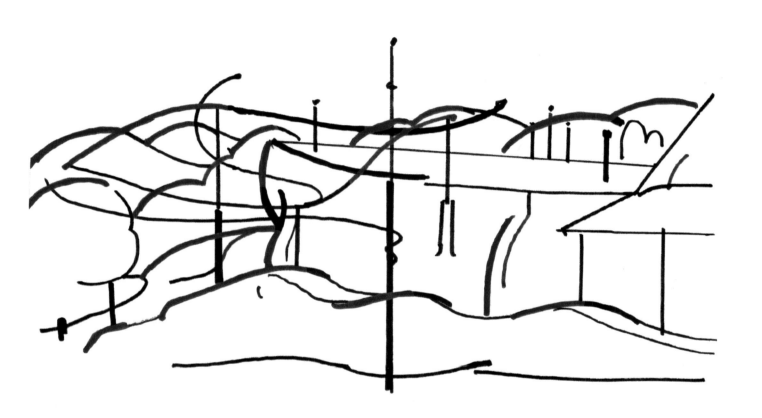

Self-similar forms at a series of connected scales.

In our emerging sustainable era, human artifacts will be seen once again as a part of a beautiful place that occurs at a series of scales. These scales range from planetary biomes to specific on-site material and energy resources-- all part of the cyclic flows of a healthy fractal order without waste or seams.

Details. In fractal design, details take on increased importance because it is through the details that we increase the range of scales of the composition. This increases complexity and diversity to help achieve a more holistic and satisfying result. The resulting feeling of "this is right" is a universal capability we all have, if exercised.

B.2 Place
g. Conclusion

Our industrial society convinced us that place was expendable--expendable first to scientific progress, then to the concentration of wealth and finally to greed for its own sake. The effort needed to maintain place was superseded by an effort to escape place, as romanticized in the form of space exploration. Thus, space replaced place--however, space isn't a functional replacement. Place supports life while outer space does not. As the industrial era eventually transforms into the next phase of human culture, these attitudes will change.

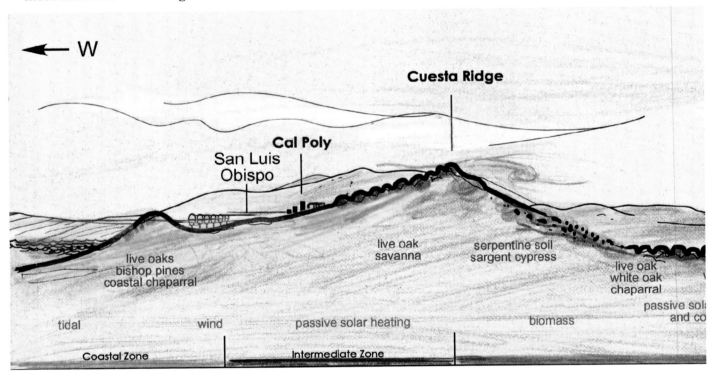

The questions from section A--Our Place in Nature, Our Population Density, Our Use of Resources, and the Question of Balance--all must be redefined in the formative phase of the emerging cultural era of information and sustainability. But, is this shift really happening? Where is the evidence? Are there real life examples available beyond flowery words, diagrams and definitions? An example dear our hearts is the place we live and work.

Below is a west to east section of San Luis Obispo County in central California. It illustrates the energy and resources this unique place can provide to a sustainable culture.

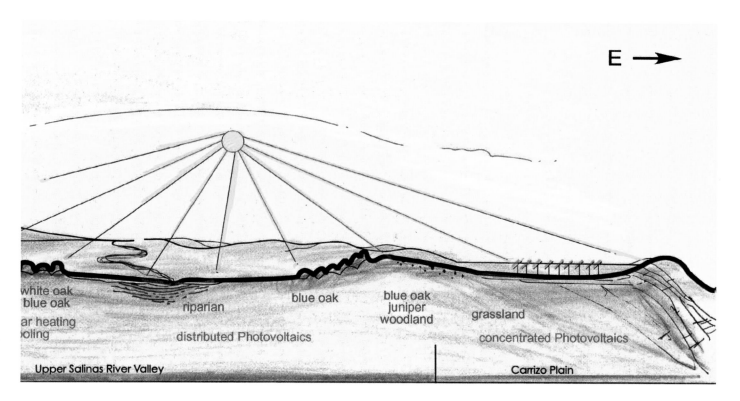

We feel privileged to be writing this in the San Luis Sustainability Group's office, which is passively heated and cooled, where all electricity used is produced onsite by photovoltaic panels and micro-hydro generation. This office is constructed of walls made of straw bales and other healthy green materials that are locally produced. It is articulated by beautiful wood milled on site after a fire killed the trees. It is surrounded by a regenerated natural landscape of often dramatic seasonal cycles and exquisite beauty. It is just one of thousands of new seeds beginning to sprout that will create a new cultural landscape, one that grows from the compost of its predecessors and is superior to the previous eras with regard to providing **health, wealth** and **equity.**

Sustainability is a word symbol that suggests deep values and intangible cultural assets. In the evolution of our species and culture, it is the latest of these symbols, applicable to our present condition with all its problems and opportunities. We are blessed to be part of this critical epochal transition in the creative dance of life.

Acknowledgements

The authors would like to thank the following people for their help on this project and their influence in developing sustainable design.

Liz Barber - for help and encouragement beyond the call of duty.

Ralph Abraham - a mathematician and author who showed that nonlinear dynamics and cultural dynamics are related.

David Bainbridge - for providing information on life-cycle energy costs, and for thirty years of inspirational work in passive solar and resource-efficient design.

Carl Bovill - for inspiring us with his book, *Fractal Geometry in Architecture and Design*.

Lynne Elizabeth - for past collaboration and for reviewing our draft of this book.

Pliny Fisk and Gale Vittori - for pushing the envelope of the theory of sustainable design, the joy of collaboration on projects and for providing examples for the life-cycle design section.

Christine Gyovai - for research, text, graphic composition and editing.

Jude Gyovai - for her eagle editing eye.

Harold Hay - for getting us involved in solar architecture many years ago.

Ryan Johnson - for graphic support.

Michael McGuire - for kindly allowing us to use material from his excellent book *An Eye for Fractals*.

Phil Niles - for years of collaboration and hard-nosed analysis to counter the tendency of us architects to rely too much on trained arrows.

Raul Arias de Para - for helping with the description and providing photographs of Canopy Tower Lodge in Panama.

Jennifer Reut - for editorial assistance.

The folks at San Luis Sustainability Group - for support, knowledge and tolerance while this book was being produced.

David Wright - for willingness to provide a final review and being an inspired pioneer in solar architecture.

Credits

Page:

INDEX